I0796992

OTHER TITLES AVAILABLE IN THIS CROCHET FAIRY TALES SERIES

Animal Fables

Castle Tales

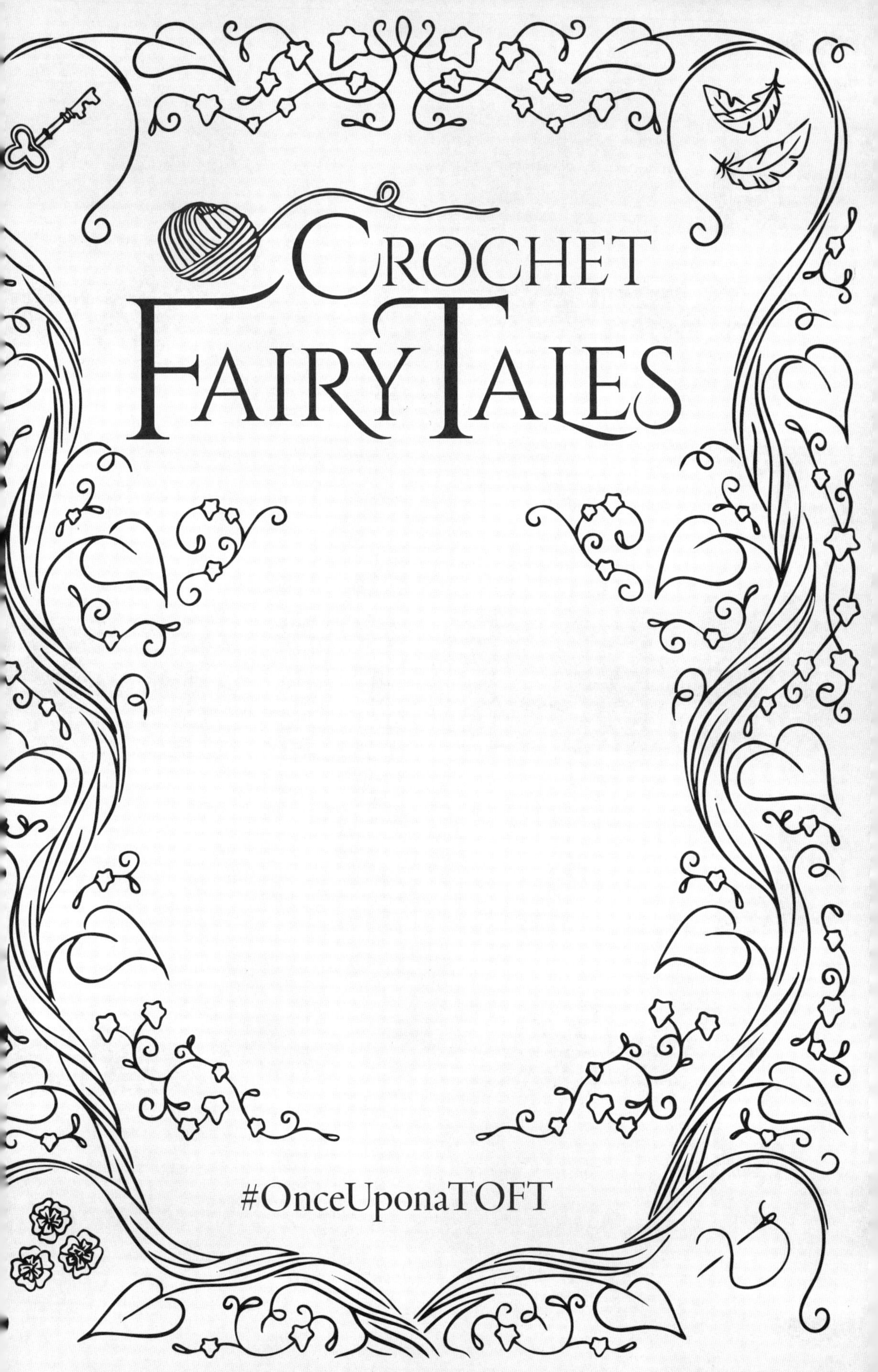

Crochet Fairy Tales

#OnceUponaTOFT

COTTAGE STORIES

Over 40 enchanting patterns

KERRY LORD

DAVID & CHARLES
—PUBLISHING—

www.davidandcharles.com

CONTENTS

PROLOGUE

THE STORIES

EPILOGUE

INTRODUCTION

Fairy tales have long cast a powerful spell over my imagination, and as an avid childhood reader with an insatiable appetite for any story involving magic, talking animals or little folk of the forest, I feel that I was somewhat destined to one day write this series of books. You are always, however, a collector rather than a writer of fairy tales, and so in my reimagining of these much-loved traditional characters I hope to instil that with some of the very special magic of crochet and retell these well-known stories in my own way.

The origin of the six fairy tales in this book are varied, woven together by having at their heart the setting of a cottage that is often, but not exclusively, found within a deep dark wood. They come from the folk traditions of German, Danish and English, and with the exception of Andersen's *Thumbelina* are regarded as traditional oral rather than literary tales. Of course the most famous of all tales within this collection are the Grimm's stories of *Red Riding Hood, Snow White, Hansel and Gretel* and *Elves and the Shoemaker*. The most important and ever-popular collection of folk tales to be written down, diving into the brother Grimm's *Children's and Household Tales* was like following a long twisting path of breadcrumbs deep into the forest. The Hansel and Gretel story that I thought I knew very well was in fact just one version of the tale, and the more I read the more I uncovered curious extra details, as well as total omissions of the parts that I often found most intriguing and plot-twisting changes to characters. Throughout their lifetimes and seven editions and reprints of their work, the Grimm brothers themselves rewrote and edited the stories, reshaping them to their modern world to the point where some bear little resemblance to the original oral record. What I quickly discovered while starting to read more and more versions of the same fairy tales was that if I wished to crochet characters from them, then I would first have to write my own stories. By their very nature fairy tales shift and change with each retelling, and so I realised that before I crocheted a single stitch I would first have to design the fairy tale world for my characters to live in.

> "In this fairy tale world all the human dolls are children, as I see them as stories that centre around a child or children and what happens to them."

In my retelling of these stories I have chosen to tread a path between the more traditional darkness and the modern sweetness of children's tales. I have picked and chosen between the details of the oldest and newest retellings, not dwelling over the ever-impending threat of birds pecking your eyes out, but also making sure that it's not always just step-mothers who are evil. Both appropriate to read to your children but with some details that those who have not read these tales for decades will find engaging. In this tradition of the ever-changing fairy tale I have chosen to include certain accessories or scenery and even add to the stories so that they perform as I need them to with my crocheted retelling. I have not put characters in modern settings, nor have I worried about capturing accurate historical detail, and where I have edited the plots of any stories it was to accentuate the important details and omit anything superfluous or even entire characters who don't lend themselves towards being crocheted.

In this fairy tale world all the human dolls are children, as I see them as stories that centre around a child or children and what happens to them. Snow White is depicted as she was when turning seven when her step-mother first became aware of her beauty, Jack is just about big enough to wield an axe, but not old enough to not be tempted by the promise of magic beans, and Red Riding Hood is certainly too naive to be wandering around unchaperoned where big bad wolves might find her. All the human adult characters are absent from the patterns, supporting the crocheted child protagonists in the narrative of what happens to them, but not being created in yarn themselves. Like the elves and fairies the dwarves of my tales are not human, and so take on their own standard body shape and scale away from that of the human children. When the human characters and thus the reader gets to know the magical characters then they have names, whereas the mysterious elves that help the shoemaker and his wife remain anonymous.

In my fairy tales the animals are all anthropomorphised in both their shapes and characters, although I've also been very careful to retain their ability to transform back onto four legs rather than just always walk on two. As I view the big bad wolf he needs to induce the physical fear that you'd feel when face to face with the real animal in a forest, while also prompting the uncomfortable and unsafe physiological reaction to finding yourself having wandered off the path alone with a stranger who you suddenly realise is far older and stronger than you. Animals can speak, and choose to wear clothes when it suits them to do so. In this particular collection of fairy tales birds are very symbolically important, carrying four of the characters to safety and freedom. Birds are friends of children: Hansel and Gretel sit upon the duck's back to cross the river back home, Jack rides upon the giant's chicken as fast as he can down the beanstalk to secure his and his mother's future, and Thumbelina's dear friend the swallow flies her far away to a new life to find her happily ever after.

> "If a fairy tale is a story of transformation, then this crocheted retelling where balls of yarn become the characters within those tales is surely the most magical."

I have viewed these crochet dolls as being both for adults and for children throughout the process of writing both the stories and crocheting the shapes. In order to recreate the scenes that you see on these pages we have used modelling wire within the limbs and some scenery to make the characters and their props self-support. This is easy for you to do yourself should you wish to create a scene within a bookshelf in your home or where Jack's beanstalk could grow from your mantelpiece or Thumbelina could perch upon her swallow on your window sill. However, if you are making these for a child to play with then keep them safe by making them without the addition of any wire or wooden sticks. It is my hope that by my giving you all of the techniques and theory of creating hairstyles, that some children might indeed be made as the protagonists of their own fairy tales. I'm sure plenty of children would love to be depicted as Thumbelina and her flower fairy friends or even as the brave siblings Hansel and Gretel. Beyond the characterisation within these stories I also hope that some will be creative enough to use the patterns as a blueprint for making dolls far beyond the pages of this book. Together across all the human characters in these stories you have the patterns for mini doll clothes that could very easily be tweaked so you'd be able to create perfect portraits of all the people you know.

In addition to the hope that some of these dolls might walk right off the page and live beyond their fairy tales, I have deliberately chosen Christmas as the setting of the only elves in my collection, meaning that these magical little folk lend themselves to becoming part of your festive decorations. They'd be just as at-home helping Santa out building toys as they would be hammering the nails into the soles of the shoemaker's boots. It's very easy to imagine an entire army of little elfin helpers hidden around your house in the countdown to Christmas, each one finished with different hats, hairstyles and shoes from right across the whole book. Equally the pieces of scenery and accessories have been designed to work far beyond the stories. Make the toadstool Thumbelina shelters under for Halloween, the Golden Egg for Easter, or dress up the pine trees in which Gretel and Hansel are abandoned for Christmas.

While wandering around off the path that leads to the mountains in my newly imagined fairyland I stumbled across another incredibly creative hobby I had long forgotten, and fell freshly head over heels with miniatures. When made in TOFT fine yarn on a 2mm hook (for US crocheters: sport/4ply on an A) – see Thumbelina on the front inside cover – the characters and their accessories in this book will all be 12th scale, which is the most common dolls house scale, perfect for using with additional dolls house furniture and accessories. In the pages of this book you will spot a few perfectly formed little props that have been gathered from sometimes very old, occasionally brand new and often craftily handmade dolls houses.

If you've read this far in my introduction then I'm sure you will love the other books in the Crochet Fairy Tales series. *Animal Fables* tackles the stories where animals come in trios! Think the billy goats, three pigs, and the sole human character of that collection – Goldilocks and the three bears. The third title explores the world of princesses, one in which some little girls are imprisoned in tall towers with no stairs, others in underwater kingdoms made of coral and most of them share the dream of living out their happily ever after inside a castle.

If a fairy tale is a story of transformation, then this crocheted retelling where balls of yarn become the characters within those tales is surely the most magical. When crocheting your version of these patterns you are in fact going to become the next reteller of these tales, able to decide whether your Snow White will discover all seven dwarves living in a cottage in the woods, or if she in fact maybe only finds three.

Please share your own retelling of these tales using the tag #OnceuponaTOFT so that I can enjoy seeing your characters and their stories.

I hope that this book gives you many hours of escapism and creativity, whether you can already crochet and are diving right in now, or whether you will enjoy reading the stories, before you are one day tempted to pick up a hook and try your first few stitches.

On your path through this enchanting world may you find a project bag that endlessly refills with yarn so you can keep on hooking happily ever after!

Kerry Lord

How to Use This Book

Each chapter begins with a retelling of the fairy tale, followed by the patterns to recreate the story including characters, their accessories and some scenery.

The patterns within this book are created using simple crochet and embroidery stitches but in order to instil them with lots of detail there are tit-bits of lots of different techniques used in every design. As you crochet your way through each chapter you will follow your unravelling ball of yarn deep into the enchanted woods and discover new skills and satisfaction along the way.

The pages before the story chapters have been designed as a technical introduction for everyone to read before they begin crocheting from the book, whereas the technical pages that follow the stories are intended as a reference that can be used as you are making and an essential for a less-experienced crocheter. Those who are totally new to crochet may need to rely on these pages heavily until you are familiar with the basics of the double crochet stitch, and I would recommend starting your crochet story by making the Golden Egg to master how to start, increasing and decreasing (*see Reading a Pattern*).

With many of the dolls you will be stuffing and sewing them up as you progress through the pattern in order to add surface details onto their clothes. This will be highlighted within the pattern with this needle and thread symbol and means you will need to stuff and sew up what you have made so far or you will likely miss details such as collars or cuffs. For a general guide to stuffing and sewing up the doll and other shapes see *Stuffing & Sewing Up*.

I have used British English crochet terms throughout. 'Double crochet' (dc) is the American English 'single crochet' (sc). For clarification on all the US term as what they refer to please see the table below.

UK		US	
ch	chain	ch	chain
sl st	slip stitch	sl st	slip stitch
dc	double crochet	sc	single crochet
dc2tog	dc 2 together	sc2tog	sc 2 together
htr	half treble crochet	hdc	half double crochet
tr	treble crochet	dc	double crochet
dtr	double treble crochet	tr	treble crochet
ttr	triple treble crochet	dtr	double treble crochet

The Story of TOFT

A Well-Spun Tale

I first felt like I was spinning straw into gold back in 2006 when I founded my British yarn company TOFT and have had the pleasure of creating an ever-expanding range of luxury natural wools ever since. Having then knitted away on hats and scarves for six years I crocheted my first stitch in 2012. Discovering 3D crochet ignited my creativity in a way that I could not have ever imagined was possible. With the simple cubic building block of the double crochet stitch it is possible to create every shape imaginable and with it sculpt yarn into whatever you wish for. This collection of patterns is the most ambitious creative project TOFT has ever undertaken, and although many elements of the crochet patterns themselves remain simple and reliant upon basic techniques, the combination of embroidery stitches and more surface crochet elevate the finished items with so much more detail than we have ever achieved before. Even the most advanced crocheter is likely to learn a thing or two as they work through the projects in this book, from how to embroider a French knot through to the fiddly technical witchcraft of creating 'invisible rows'.

When crocheted in TOFT pure wool this book's characters and their story's scenery are soft and supple with movement and character and remain incredibly tactile. Creating a closed dense fabric is not harsh upon your hands when working in a wool as the bounce in the yarn is incredibly forgiving on tension and so you do not need to be concerned about maintaining a very tight tension to avoid seeing your stuffing. Using TOFT's natural fibres is not only better for the environment, but you will achieve a beautiful finish and will never need to compromise on your choice of colours while creating your retelling of any of these stories. TOFT yarns are fibre dyed rather than flat dyed and this means that many of our colours are made by mixing complicated blends of shades together so that the stitches you make have crisp definition, true depth, and will last for decades.

TOFT spins pure wool yarns in four different weights, and for each you would use a different size hook. These magical toadstools are made using exactly the same pattern worked in a fine, double knitting, aran and chunky weight of yarn. The character, accessory and scenery patterns in this book can be used with any thickness of yarn you wish, matching your hook size accordingly, and as you play with this idea of scale you will be able to create both immaculately perfect miniature fairylands or the oversized realm of the giants.

TOFT is a real place in Warwickshire, England and we are always here to help you if you are new to crochet and you don't know where to begin. Videos are also available to accompany all the techniques used in this book and can be found along with all the materials at **www.toftuk.com**.

Yarn & Tools

All the exact yarn, additional materials and tools I have used to create this book are available from TOFT, from fairy tale stitch markers to modelling wire and even wooden dowels.

YARN

These fairy tales have been created using a palette of just twelve bright colours (opposite), combined with TOFT's original twelve natural shades *(see Characterisation)*. From the top left in rows these are Peony, Lime, Yellow, Sage, Chive, Orange, Hyacinth, Green, Ruby, Sapphire, Kale and Beetroot. In many ways I have chosen a very classic colour palette, inspired by the beautifully detailed watercolour illustrations of so many of the early and later fairy tale books you read. The prominence of the primary colours Ruby, Yellow and Blue retains a child-friendly tone in the photography but when added to the complexity of the blended natural colours, three pastels and four deep greens the palette becomes everything you need to depict even the most sophisticated of tales.

The patterns photographed in this book have all been created using TOFT's pure wool double knit yarn on a 3mm hook with the exception of the magical toadstools *(see The Story of TOFT)* (for US crocheters: light worsted/8ply on a C2 or D3). The human characters in these stories are all children, and when worked in a TOFT double knit weight yarn their completed height from head to toe (before working any hair) is 19cm (7½in).

The quantity of double knitting yarn you require has been stated both to create the whole story including all the extra narrative scenery and accessories, and also on each individual piece within a story so you can opt just to create the protagonist if you wish. Where accessories share colours with the characters and yarn quantities allow I have made the full story ingredients more efficient so you will need fewer 25g balls to complete the project. When using other yarns please be aware that the quantities may vary significantly depending on the fibre composition of the yarn you use. For example, a cotton yarn will be heavier and so you'll need much more whereas an acrylic will be lighter and so you'll require less.

HOOK

Using the right sized hook to match your yarn and create the correct tension is vital for ensuring the best results. Adjust your hook size to match the yarn and accommodate your tension. If your hook is too big your stitches will be loose and stuffing will show through, whereas if it is too tight you will find the pieces you make are stiff and some of the smaller details in these patterns very difficult to work. If you are purchasing a hook for the first time choose one with a comfortable larger handle as it will double as the perfect tool for pushing stuffing inside small pieces such as arms and legs.

STITCH MARKER

Marking the start or end of each round with something is essential in this style of crochet as the vast majority of the time we are working in a non-stop spiral where these end of rounds become essentially invisible *(see Technicals)*.

TOFT

CENTRALISER

In the odd pattern there will also be a call to place an additional traditional stitch marker, referred to as a centraliser, in order to identify a point in the piece for the construction or to help with sewing up. These are then removed once the piece is complete.

SCISSORS

Sharp scissors or thread snips will be essential for snipping off the ends of yarn at the surface of the fabric once you have secured them.

STUFFING

Several different types of stuffing are available including natural pure wool and recycled polyester options. If you are making these as toys for children I would recommend a polyester so they can be washed by hand or in a cool machine cycle.

SEWING NEEDLE

For some of the embroidery detail in these projects you might find a slim tapestry needle gives you a little more accuracy than a traditional larger one – just ensure that your yarn will fit through the eye with ease.

CONTRAST YARN OR SAFETY EYES

I have chosen to add all eyes by embroidering with black lengths of yarn. Small safety eyes could be used as an alternative and would need to be added before the gathering of the stitches on the head. Do not use safety eyes on anything made for a child under five.

PINS FOR SEWING UP

If you are new to 3D crochet you might find pins are useful for positioning parts before you do the final few stitches to sew them up.

DOWELS OR TWIGS

In lots of the accessories, such as axes and hammers, I have used wooden dowels inside the crochet. These should not be used on pieces given to young children and instead just leave them out and add stuffing as an alternative. Hansel and Gretel's camp-fire also uses real twigs which are not intended as a toy and so in this instance crochet several of the handles from the elves' hammer as a substitute.

MODELLING WIRE

If you wish to recreate some of the scenes in this book to display the characters in your home on your mantelpiece or book shelf, then you may wish to add a soft aluminium modelling wire to them. Wiring the legs and arms of dolls will allow you to position them to capture a moment in the story; it enables chickens to stand, tulips to open and dwarves to lift their arms to strike their pickaxes. This is only ever to be used when they are not intended to be toys and is in no way essential to the making of any of the characters or accessories.

GLASSES

The big bad wolf completes his disguise with the addition of Grandma's glasses. These are available to purchase, or could be made using the modelling wire.

Characterisation

Reimagine and create the protagonist of your favourite fairy tale exactly how you have always seen them in your mind's eye.

Skin Tones and Hair Colours

TOFT's twelve-colour natural palette is perfect for recreating people and animals (both human and mythical ones!) From the top left in rows these are Stone, Oatmeal, Cream, Steel, Shale, Silver, Chestnut, Fudge, Camel, Charcoal, Cocoa and Mushroom.

The skin tones and hair colours that I have used to create my characters are stated 'as shown' at the start of the individual patterns. With the exception perhaps of Snow White, these fairy tales do not make reference to the appearance of a character, leaving the canvas blank for you to reimagine and make them exactly as you wish. When deciding upon hair colours remember that more that one can be combined in a hairstyle, especially if you combine the greys in a gradient or use a couple of the lighter shades in combination with a brown to suggest highlights.

If you are trying to recreate people that you know then I would advise selecting your skin tones and hair colours and then consider also changing the colours of a character's clothing to match an outfit or favourite colour of that person. With the exception of Red Riding Hood's cloak there is no description in the fairy tales that talks about the colour of clothing, and so there is nothing stopping you recreating Gretel's dress in pinks or Thumbelina in purple if you wish.

Hairstyles

Add the hair to your doll once they are stuffed and sewn up. All of the techniques overleaf would work for both short and long styles. It is often easiest to mark out the hairline first before filling in the scalp afterwards. For all hairstyles the specifics of how I have made each character are stated in the patterns, but use the technique guides to be able to customise your dolls. See *Finishing Techniques* for a detailed step-by-step guide to the techniques.

KNOT LENGTHS

Knotting on lengths of yarn is in many ways the easiest way of adding hair to your doll. Remember to knot them on longer than you wish to trim them down to, especially if styling the hair afterwards, such as plaiting or tying up. You do not need to knot them as densely as you might think and leave two stitch gaps between them, especially on longer hair.

Technique used on Snow White.

SLIP CHAINS

Perfect for creating both long and short straight hair. Slip stitch to begin and then chain to the desired length of hair before turning and slip stitching back down the chain. When you reach the scalp slip stitch two stitches away and repeat until the head is covered. For best results vary the chain length at the back to be shorter in short styles.

Technique used on Jack.

CROCHETED CHAINS

Great for wavy and curly hair, be conscious of the right side and wrong side of your chain so that the strands curve downwards around the head. Slip stitch into the scalp in the middle of the forehead and work a parting line from front to back and then turn and work the other side before securing into place to cover the scalp. Add extra strands to achieve full coverage.

Technique used on Red Riding Hood.

CHAIN LOOPS

An easy method for creating styled hair such as braids or pigtails along with short coverage and custom facial hair. See *Beards*.

To create a pony tail or pigtails identify the point on the head that the hair would be 'tied'. Chain backwards and forwards between this point and slipping around the hairline until the scalp is completely covered. Once covered chain long lengths without slipping, three for a braid etc.

Technique used on Hansel, Gretel, Thumbelina and the elves.

BEARDS

All four different methods of adding hair to your doll can be worked for other facial hair. When working a beard complete or embroider the nose into place first. Beneath the nose work a short line of your chosen technique (for example 4cm (1½in) KNOT LENGTHS, or chain five SLIP CHAINS OR CHAIN LOOPS) to create a moustache regardless of the length of your main beard. Beneath this moustache leave a gap of two rounds of stitches in the middle to represent a mouth before then working the full beard 'ear to ear' across the rounds either side and then below. For distinguished magical beards, the kind you might find on a wizard, vary the length of the chains from short on the sides to longer in the middle to create a triangular shape.

EYEBROWS

Similarly to beards, all the hair methods can be used to add eyebrows in place. Embroider the eyes into position first before adding the eyebrows one round above the top of the eye.

Technique used on the dwarves and the elves.

Stuffing & Sewing Up

When you have finished crocheting a part the pattern will instruct you to 'Break yarn.' Whenever doing so, unless it is otherwise stated, leave a 20cm (8in) length of yarn attached so that you can sew up without needing to rejoin any yarn, and then pull the loop straight off the hook through the stitch to secure it. If a part requires you to stuff or sew up before you progress to the next step then this will always be stated in the pattern, but otherwise this can be done at the end once the piece is fully complete. Follow the *Gathering Stitches* steps below if the pattern instructs you to break yarn, stuff and gather stitches.

DWARVES

The shared body pattern of the dwarves is made by first creating two legs, and then joining the legs together to directly move on to crocheting the body and head off the top of the legs. In the same way the noses are either crocheted on or rejoined to be crocheted directly onto the face rather than sewn on separately. This means that there is very little sewing in the construction as the whole of the legs, body and head form one cavity that you need to stuff. Add stuffing to the hands leaving the arms unstuffed before sewing onto the body separately.

ANIMALS

The wolf is made by crocheting two feet which are rejoined to become legs which you then crochet together at the top to continue directly onto the torso leaving holes for the arms. The head and ears are made separately to the body and I would recommend sewing the head onto the top of the gathered neck first before then adding the ears and sewing the eyes and nose. The birds are sewn up by adding a little stuffing to the top of their legs before sewing in place on the bottom of the bodies towards the back so that if they are not wired they will sit with their legs splaying forwards. As with the dolls, add any extra features or detailing first before adding the eyes last.

GATHERING STITCHES

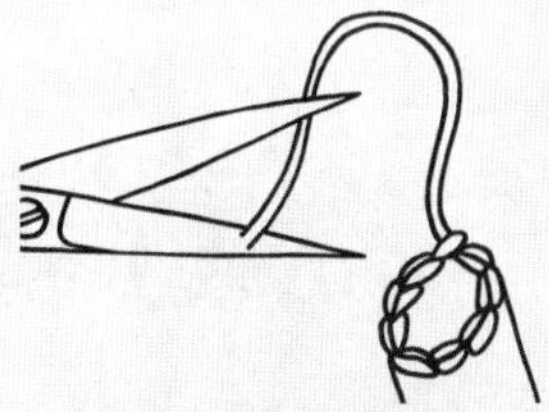

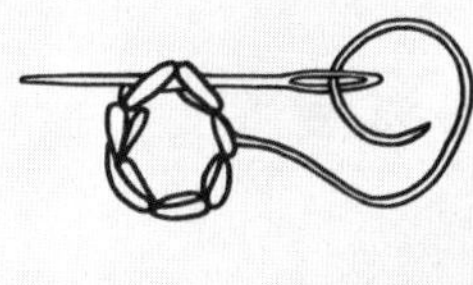

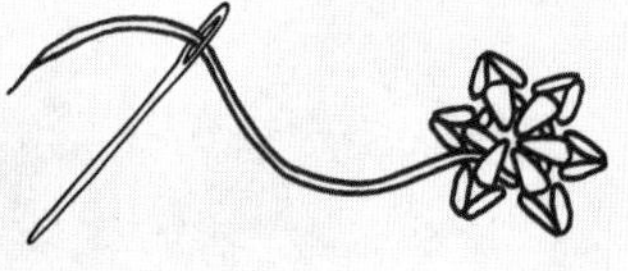

1. Fasten off the last stitch of the round by cutting the yarn and pulling the tail through the remaining loop and stuff the piece if stated in the pattern.
2. Thread the end of the yarn onto a sewing needle and sew a running stitch through all the remaining stitches of the round.
3. Pull tightly to gather and close the stitches, then fasten off into the fabric around a stitch.

DOLLS

All the human characters in these stories are children and share the same pattern to keep them in scale with each other. These are made by crocheting a body and head from the bottom up in one piece with decreasing and increasing to create a neck. The limbs are crocheted separately and then sewn on, which means that they sit more naturally should you wish not to wire or add stands to them and instead leave them to sit self-supported on a shelf. When stuffing the pieces, whether a doll, animal or scenery, but especially with the characters who wear clothes, you are aiming to lightly fill out the shapes that you have made, rather than fill the pieces up with as much as you can until they become stiff or rigid. Push the stuffing down into the pieces using the handle of your hook. On the mini doll shape shown opposite you will only need to add stuffing to the feet and hands, leaving the legs and arms flat in order for them to fold nicely at their side or under their bottoms when they sit. I would always recommend the order of sewing with a mini doll to be to add the limbs first then work any hair directly onto the stuffed and sewn up shape. Finally sew the nose and then the eyes into position.

EYES AND NOSE

Using LONG STITCH add the nose and eyes to your doll last as the finishing magic-touch that will bring them to life. I would recommend sewing the nose into place first using a length of the skin tone you have used to crochet the doll. Sew a long stitch horizontally in the centre of the face around two stitches for a small nose and up to five stitches for a wide nose. Sew as many wraps of the yarn around these stitches as you wish in order to create a nose that stands off the face. Next, using a black length of yarn, add the eyes vertically either side of the nose. The personality and emotion on the face of your doll can alter dramatically with the placement of the eyes and just one stitch can make a big difference. As standard I have used two wraps of black in a yarn of equal thickness to that which I have crocheted in, wrapped twice around two rounds of stitches that end in the same round as the nose.

DRESSING

To dress and undress the mini dolls you are always best to bring their feet through the necklines of any jumpers or tunics. They have much larger heads than they do torsos and so all clothing is designed and intended to be put on from the bottom upwards before pushing the arms through any sleeves.

WIRING

In order to position the characters and some of the scenery for the photography of this book we have used a soft modelling wire within the pieces. This can be added at the end once all the stuffing, sewing up and finishing is complete, and for the best results use long single pieces that reach, for example, up one leg and then down the other, or through the body from hand to hand in one piece. Fold over the ends either side to avoid sharp tips that will push though your fabric. Of course, this is not at all suitable if you are intending to give what you have crocheted to a child of any age to play with, and is instead intended to allow you to display your creations on a shelf. If you are making Jack's beanstalk for a child to play with then sew all the vines to each other for it to stand, and replace all wooden dowels and sticks with stuffing and use removable doll stands if you wish the dolls to stand up.

TOFT
TOFT

Reading a Pattern

Even if you are a very experienced crocheter, I would recommend giving this page a glance over before you begin if you are new to TOFT patterns. In addition see *Abbreviations* for a full guide and you can refer to any of the step-by-step stitches in the back if you are unsure. If working a specific stitch or technique it will appear in CAPS and step-by-steps for these can be found in *The Stitches*.

Thumbelina's Wing

CHARTS

The only chart in this book is to help you make Thumbelina's wing *(see Thumbelina)* as the vast majority of the crochet in the book is 3D using just the double crochet stitch and so is not charted. The diagram below can be used in conjunction with the full pattern words on the page to help you visualise what you are making. Using the key follow the graphic from the starting chain. If crocheting left-handed the chart would be worked in mirror. A new row or round is indicated by a change of colour in the chart.

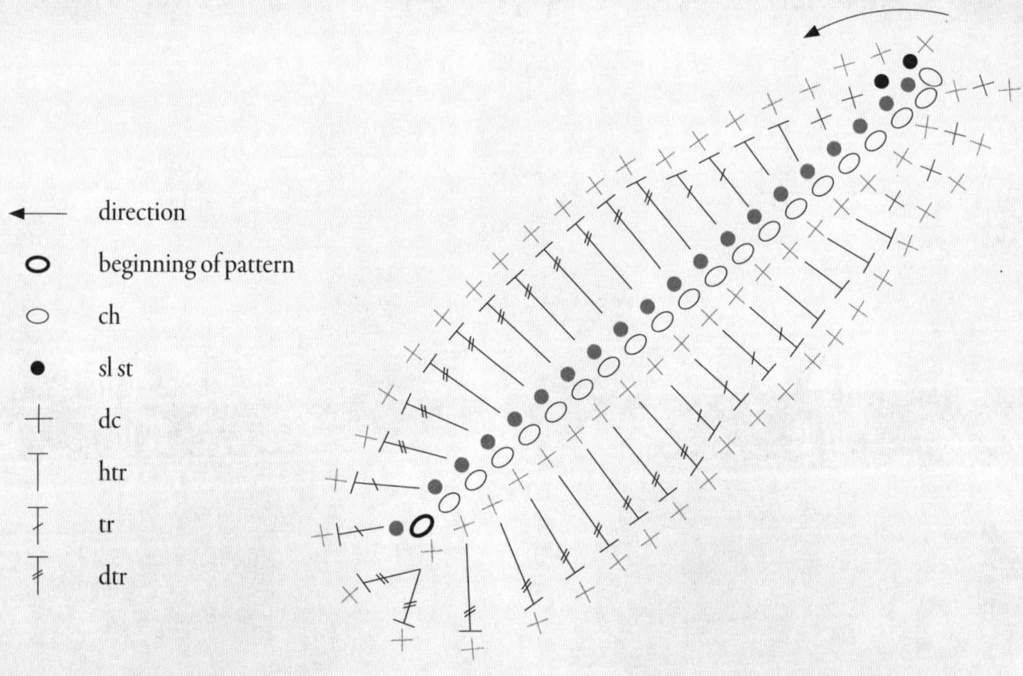

GOLDEN EGG

TO CREATE THIS ACCESSORY YOU WILL NEED

25g Yellow

See image in Jack & the Beanstalk

Working in Yellow

Begin by dc6 into ring

Rnd 1 (dc2 into next st) 6 times (12)

Rnd 2 (dc1, dc2 into next st) 6 times (18)

Rnd 3 (dc2, dc2 into next st) 6 times (24)

Rnd 4 dc

Rnd 5 (dc3, dc2 into next st) 6 times (30)

Rnds 6-9 dc (4 rnds)

Rnd 10 (dc3, dc2tog) 6 times (24)

Rnds 11-13 dc (3 rnds)

Rnd 14 (dc2, dc2tog) 6 times (18)

Rnds 15-16 dc (2 rnds)

Rnd 17 (dc1, dc2tog) 6 times (12)

Break yarn.

Stuff and gather remaining stitches to close.

RND: ROUND

A round is a complete rotation in a spiral back to where you started. In this style of crochet you DO NOT slip stitch at the end of a round to make a circle, but instead continue directly onto the next round in a spiral.

DC2 INTO NEXT ST

An increase by working two double crochet stitches into the same stitch.

DC2TOG: DOUBLE CROCHET TWO TOGETHER

This is a decrease that reduces your stitch count by double crocheting into just the front of the next two stitches to turn them into one.

STS: STITCHES

The number in brackets at the end of a line indicates the number of stitches in that round once it has been completed.

DC: DOUBLE CROCHET

'dc2' means to double crochet one stitch into the next stitch and then another double crochet stitch into the following one (not an increase).

6 TIMES

Repeat what comes directly before this instruction within the parentheses the number of times stated.

2 RNDS

Work one double crochet stitch into every stitch in the round for two full rounds.

The Stories

CHAPTER ONE

Red Riding Hood

Once upon a time there was a little girl who was loved by all who met her, but most of all by her dear old grandmother. She was fondly called 'Red Riding Hood', for she was only ever seen wearing her ruby red cloak.

One day upon hearing her grandmother was feeling ill and weak, her mother asked her to put on her favourite cloak and take some cake and wine to her cottage deep in the woods.

"Be sure to take care and stick to the path all the way," her mother called after her as she pulled up her hood and started upon her walk.

Then just as the path started to lead in-between the trees, she met a wolf. Naive to the wicked ways of a wolf, little Red Riding Hood was not at all afraid to see him and smiled widely as he came closer.

"Good day Red Riding Hood," he said. "Where are you off to in such a hurry?"

"Good day to you, too." she replied. "I'm off to visit my grandmother."

"...and where does she live?" the sly wolf enquired with a crooked smile.

"This path takes me all the way deep into the woods to her cottage," she replied.

The wolf thought to himself, *what a tasty young plump morsel she will make, far better to eat than the old woman. I shall be crafty as can be and catch both.*

Walking alongside her on the path he pointed to a far off clearing exclaiming just how pretty the flowers are that can be found growing there.

"Why don't you enjoy the joy of the woods as you walk Red Riding Hood? The smell of the flowers and the songs of the birds."

Raising her eyes from the path and pushing back her hood, she suddenly saw the beauty of the sunshine and carpet of flowers growing beneath the trees. Believing that flowers would help cheer up her grandmother she skipped off the path to pick them, but with each new stem she added to her hand she headed further from the path.

As soon as the girl had taken a dozen steps towards the flowers the wolf quickly skulked away along the path leading directly to her grandmother's cottage.

When he knocked on the door the wolf heard a distant voice call, "Who is it?"

"It's me, Grandmother, Red Riding Hood," he replied. "I've come with some cake to make you better."

"Lift the latch and come right in," said the grandmother, "for I'm too weak to lift the latch."

Without wasting a moment the wolf opened the door, ran straight to the grandmother's bed and devoured her in one huge bite. Somewhat replete but still looking forward to his main meal, he put on the grandmother's nightgown and cap, drew the curtains and climbed into her bed to wait for a knock on the door.

Meanwhile Red Riding Hood was enjoying the woods so much that she picked flowers until she could carry no more and had gradually made her way through the wood to the cottage. Finding the door ajar she had a very strange feeling, but having received no reply she pushed it open and swallowed down her uncertainty as she stepped inside.

"Good morning," she chirped as she walked straight across the room to her grandmother's bed. There she found her grandmother with her floral night cap pulled down over her face, looking altogether very strange indeed.

"Oh Grandmother, what big ears you have."

"All the better to hear you with my child," replied the wolf.

"Oh Grandmother, what big eyes you have."

"All the better to see you with my dear," smirked the wolf.

"Oh but Grandmother, what big teeth you have."

"The better to eat you with..."

Almost before the words left his mouth, the wolf leapt out of bed and swallowed up Red Riding Hood so she was never to be seen again. His aching hunger finally sated the big bad wolf climbed back into Grandmother's bed, pulled up the blankets and drifted off to sleep.

Patterns in this Story

Red Riding Hood

Basket of Cake & Wine

Wolf

Posy of Flowers

Grandmother's Nightwear

To Create the Full Story You Will Need

25g Skin Tone

25g Hair Colour

75g Shale, 75g Cream, 50g Steel, 25g Peony, 25g Silver, 25g Ruby, 25g Hyacinth, 25g Camel, 25g Stone, 25g Beetroot, 25g Lime

Doll Glasses

Red Riding Hood

TO CREATE THIS CHARACTER YOU WILL NEED

25g Skin Tone (Oatmeal), 25g Hair Colour (Fudge), 25g Ruby, 25g Cream, 25g Hyacinth, 25g Camel

Body & Head

Working in Cream

Ch6 and work around chain as follows:

Rnd 1 dc4, dc2 into next st along one side of chain, dc4, dc2 into next st along other side of chain (12)

Rnd 2 (dc2 into next st) 12 times (24)

Rnds 3-8 dc (6 rnds)

Rnd 9 (dc4, dc2tog) 4 times (20)

Rnd 10 dc

Rnd 11 (dc4, dc2 into next st) 4 times (24)

Rnds 12-15 dc (4 rnds)

Rnd 16 (dc2tog) 4 times, dc3, (dc2tog) 4 times, dc3, dc2tog (15)

Change to Skin Tone

Rnd 17 (dc2tog) 7 times, dc1 (8)

Rnd 18 dc

Rnd 19 dc2, dc3 into next st, dc5 (10)

Rnd 20 dc2 into next st, dc2, (dc2 into next st) 3 times, dc2, dc2 into next st, dc1 (15)

Rnd 21 (dc2 into next st) 15 times (30)

Rnds 22-23 dc (2 rnds)

Rnd 24 dc12, (dc2tog) four times, dc10 (26)

Rnds 25-30 dc (6 rnds)

Rnd 31 (dc2tog) 13 times (13)

Rnd 32 (dc2tog) 6 times, dc1 (7)

Stuff and gather remaining stitches to close.

Arms (make two)

Working in Skin Tone

Begin by dc6 into ring

Rnd 1 (dc1, dc2 into next st) 3 times (9)

Rnds 2-5 dc (4 rnds)

Rnd 6 (dc1, dc2tog) 3 times (6)

Rnds 7-11 dc (5 rnds)

Change to Cream

Rnd 12 dc2 into next st, dc5 (7)

Rnds 13-14 dc (2 rnds)

Rnd 15 dc2 into next, dc6 (8)

Rnds 16-20 dc (5 rnds)

Stuff hand and sew flat across top to close.

> “Her mother asked her to put on her favourite cloak and take some cake and wine to her cottage deep in the woods.”

Legs (make two)

Working in Cream

Ch9 and work around chain as follows:

Rnd 1 dc7, dc2 into next st along one side of chain, dc7, dc2 into next st along other side of chain (18)

Rnds 2-3 dc (2 rnds)

Rnd 4 (dc2tog) 3 times, dc6, (dc2tog) 3 times (12)

Rnd 5 (dc2tog) twice, dc4, (dc2tog) twice (8)

Rnds 6-8 dc (3 rnds)

Rnd 9 dc2 into next st, dc4 Cream, dc3 Skin Tone (9)

Continue in Skin Tone

Rnds 10-12 dc (3 rnds)

Rnd 13 dc2 into next st, dc8 (10)

Rnds 14-15 dc (2 rnds)

Stuff foot and sew flat across top to close.

Sew up your doll *(see Stuffing & Sewing Up)*.

Sew eyes into place with Black yarn and nose with Skin Tone yarn.

Working in Hair Colour use CROCHETED CHAINS, working ch19 and sl st 4, dc2 into next st, sl st 13 back down chain *(see Hairstyles)*.

Cuffs - working in Cream, htr2 into each st around the colour change line on each arm.

Socks - working in Cream, htr2 into each st around the colour change line on each leg.

Collar - working in Cream, sl st into centre front of neckline, 2 rnds down from colour change and tr18 around the colour change line with right side facing upwards.

Hair Bow

Working in Hyacinth

Ch31 and sl st 30 back down chain

Tie into a bow and sew into position on hair.

Skirt

Working in Hyacinth

Ch20 and sl st to join into a circle

Rnd 1 dc

Change to Cream

Rnd 2 (dc4, dc2 into next st) 4 times (24)

Rnd 3 dc

Change to Hyacinth

Rnd 4 (dc3, dc2 into next st) 6 times (30)

Rnds 5-7 dc (3 rnds)

Rnd 8 (dc4, dc2 into next st) 6 times (36)

Rnds 9-11 dc (3 rnds)

Change to Cream

Rnd 12 (dc5, dc2 into next st) 6 times (42)

Rnd 13 dc

Rnd 14 (dc2 into next st) 42 times (84)

Break yarn.

Working in Hyacinth, work a round of htr around the colour change line at bottom of skirt.

Place skirt onto doll and sew into position to secure.

Belt

Working in Camel

Ch24 and sl st to join into a circle

Break yarn and sew around waist.

Bow

Working in Cream

Ch31 and dc30 back down chain

Tie into a bow and sew in position on centre back of belt.

Shoes (make two)

Working in Camel

Ch9 and work around chain as follows:

Rnd 1 dc7, dc2 into next st along one side of chain, dc7, dc2 into next st along other side of chain (18)

Rnd 2 dc2 into next st, dc15, dc2 into next st, dc1 (20)

Rnd 3 dc

Rnd 4 dc2tog, dc14, (dc2tog) twice (17)

Continue to work the straps as follows:

sl st 14, ch2, miss 3, tr1, ch2, miss 3, sl st 1

Break yarn.

Cloak

Working in Ruby

Begin by dc6 into ring

Rnd 1 (dc1, dc2 into next st) 3 times (9)

Rnd 2 (dc2, dc2 into next st) 3 times (12)

Rnd 3 (dc3, dc into next st) 3 times (15)

Rnd 4 (dc4, dc2 into next st) 3 times (18)

Rnd 5 dc

Rnd 6 (dc5, dc2 into next st) 3 times (21)

Rnd 7 dc

Rnd 8 (dc6, dc2 into next st) 3 times (24)

Rnd 9 dc

Rnd 10 (dc7, dc2 into next st) 3 times (27)

Rnd 11 (dc8, dc2 into next st) 3 times (30)

Continue to work the next 24 sts in rows as follows, using INVISIBLE ROWS technique on wrong side rows if desired:

Row 1 (RS) (dc3, dc2 into next st) 6 times, turn (30)

Row 2 (WS) (INV) dc30, turn

Row 3 (RS) (dc4, dc2 into next st) 6 times, turn (36)

Row 4 (WS) (INV) dc36, turn

Row 5 (RS) dc36

Break yarn.

With the right side of the hood facing you, create a 16-st row along the bottom by dc5 along the edge of the hood rows, dc6 along hood, dc5 along the edge of the rows.

Continue to work this 16-st row as follows to create the back of the cloak:

Row 1 (WS) (INV) dc16, turn

Row 2 (RS) (dc2 into next st) 16 times, turn (32)

Row 3 (WS) (INV) dc32, turn

Row 4 (RS) (dc2 into next st) twice, dc28, (dc2 into next st) twice, turn (36)

Row 5 (WS) (INV) dc36, turn

Row 6 (RS) (dc2 into next st) 3 times, dc30, (dc2 into next st) 3 times, turn (42)

Row 7 (WS) (INV) dc42, turn

Row 8 (RS) dc42

Break yarn.

Ties - sl st into the corner between the hood and the cloak, ch19 and sl st 18 back down chain, dc around the edge of the cloak to the other side, ch19 and sl st 18 back down chain. Break yarn.

“Believing that flowers would help cheer up her grandmother she skipped off the path to pick them, but with each new stem she added to her hand she headed further from the path.”

Basket of Cake & Wine

TO CREATE THIS ACCESSORY YOU WILL NEED

25g Stone, 25g Beetroot, 25g Camel, 25g Oatmeal

Basket Outer

Working in Stone

Begin by dc6 into ring

Working into back loop

Rnd 1 (dc2 into next st) 6 times (12)

Rnd 2 (dc1, dc2 into next st) 6 times (18)

Rnd 3 (dc2, dc2 into next st) 6 times (24)

Rnd 4 (htr3, htr2 into next st) 6 times (30)

Rnds 5-7 htr (3 rnds)

Rnd 8 dc working through the whole stitch

Break yarn.

Basket Inner

Working in Stone

Begin by dc6 into ring

Rnd 1 (dc2 into next st) 6 times (12)

Rnd 2 (dc1, dc2 into next st) 6 times (18)

Rnd 3 (dc2, dc2 into next st) 6 times (24)

Break yarn and sew the inner inside the basket to create a base.

Handle - working in Stone

Sl st into top edge of basket, ch18 and sl st to opposite side, sl st 1 along edge, then dc back along chain and sl st into edge. Break yarn.

Cake Top

Working in Camel

Begin by dc6 into ring

Rnd 1 (dc2 into next st) 6 times (12)

Rnd 2 (dc1, dc2 into next st) 6 times (18)

Rnds 3-4 dc (2 rnds)

Break yarn.

Cake Base

Working in Camel

Begin by dc6 into ring

Rnd 1 (dc2 into next st) 6 times (12)

Rnd 2 (dc1, dc2 into next st) 6 times (18)

Stuff and DC JOIN the base to the top.

Working in Oatmeal, embroider a cross on top using four DAISY STITCHES.

Wine Bottle

Working in Beetroot

Begin by dc6 into ring

Rnd 1 (dc1, dc2 into next st) 3 times (9)

Working into back loop only

Rnd 2 dc

Continue working through whole stitch

Rnds 3-6 dc (4 rnds)

Rnd 7 dc2tog, dc7 (8)

Rnd 8 dc3, dc2tog, dc3 (7)

Rnd 9 dc2tog, dc5 (6)

Rnd 10 dc

Rnd 11 (dc1, dc2 into next st) 3 times (9)

Break yarn.

Stuff bottle, then working in Camel, MAKE BOBBLE (5) into the top to create the cork.

WOLF

TO CREATE THIS CHARACTER YOU WILL NEED

75g Shale, 50g Steel, 25g Silver

Centraliser

Foot One (make two)

Working in Shale

Begin by dc6 into ring

Rnd 1 (dc2 into next st) 6 times (12)

Rnd 2 dc1, ch4, miss 4, dc1, (dc1, dc2 into next st) 3 times (15)

Rnds 3-6 dc (4 rnds)

Rnd 7 (dc4, dc2 into next st) 3 times (18)

Rnds 8-9 dc (2 rnds)

Rnd 10 (dc4, dc2 into next st) 3 times, (dc2 into next st) 3 times (24)

Count 6 sts backwards, split and work these sts as follows:

Rnd 1 (dc1, dc2 into next st) 3 times (9)

Rnds 2-4 dc (3 rnds)

Break yarn.

Rejoin and work remaining 18-st rnd as follows:

Rnds 1-2 dc (2 rnds)

Split into three rnds of 6 sts and work each as follows:

Rnd 1 (dc1, dc2 into next st) 3 times (9)

Rnd 2 (dc2, dc2 into next st) 3 times (12)

Rnds 3-4 dc (2 rnds)

Rnd 5 (dc1, dc2tog) 4 times (8)

Break yarn.

Continue to work the back leg onto one of the feet. Keep the other foot safe to use later.

Back Leg One

Working in Shale

Rejoin and work 8 sts around the hole in foot (work along the front of the opening first)

Rnd 1 dc

Rnd 2 (dc2 into next st, dc3) twice (10)

Rnds 3-6 dc (4 rnds)

Rnd 7 (dc2 into next st, dc4) twice (12)

Rnd 8 dc

Rnd 9 dc4, (dc2 into next st) 3 times, dc5 (15)

Rnds 10-11 dc (2 rnds)

Rnd 12 dc4, (dc2tog) 3 times, dc5 (12)

Rnd 13 (dc5, dc2 into next st) twice (14)

Rnds 14-15 dc (2 rnds)

Rnd 16 (dc6, dc2 into next st) twice (16)

Rnds 17-18 dc (2 rnds)

Rnd 19 dc3, (dc2 into next st) 4 times, dc9 (20)

Rnd 20 dc4, dc2 into next st, dc4, place centraliser, dc2 into next st, (dc4, dc2 into next st) twice (24)

Break yarn.

Foot Two (make two)

Working in Shale

Begin by dc6 into ring

Rnd 1 (dc2 into next st) 6 times (12)

Rnd 2 dc1, ch4, miss 4, dc1, (dc1, dc2 into next st) 3 times (15)

Rnds 3-6 dc (4 rnds)

Rnd 7 (dc4, dc2 into next st) 3 times (18)

Rnds 8-9 dc (2 rnds)

Rnd 10 dc4, dc2 into next st, dc3, (dc2 into next st) 3 times, dc1, dc2 into next st, dc4, dc2 into next st (24)

dc15, count 6 sts backwards, split and work these sts as follows:

Rnd 1 (dc1, dc2 into next st) 3 times (9)

Rnds 2-3 dc (2 rnds)

Break yarn.

Rejoin and work remaining 18-st rnd as follows:

Rnds 1-2 dc (2 rnds)

Split into three rnds of 6 sts and work each as follows:

Rnd 1 (dc1, dc2 into next st) 3 times (9)

Rnd 2 (dc2, dc2 into next st) 3 times (12)

Rnds 3-4 dc (2 rnds)

Rnd 5 (dc1, dc2tog) 4 times (8)

Break yarn.

Continue to work the back leg onto one of the feet. Keep the other foot safe to use later.

Back Leg Two

Working in Shale

Rejoin and work 8 sts around the hole in the foot (front side of foot first)

Rnd 1 dc

Rnd 2 (dc2 into next st, dc3) twice (10)

Rnds 3-6 dc (4 rnds)

Rnd 7 (dc2 into next st, dc4) twice (12)

Rnd 8 dc

Rnd 9 dc5, (dc2 into next st) 3 times, dc4 (15)

Rnds 10-11 dc (2 rnds)

Rnd 12 dc5, (dc2tog) 3 times, dc4 (12)

Rnd 13 (dc2 into next st, dc5) twice (14)

Rnds 14-15 dc (2 rnds)

Rnd 16 (dc2 into next st, dc6) twice (16)

Rnd 17 dc

Rnd 18 (dc2 into next st) twice, dc12, (dc2 into next st) twice (20)

Rnd 19 (dc4, dc2 into next st) 4 times (24)

Rnd 20 dc22 (incomplete rnd)

Do not break yarn.

Stuff the back feet and legs and then continue.

Body

Working in Shale

Place the two legs next to each other with the small toes on the outside. Line up the end of your current round with the centraliser marked stitch on leg one and dc4 through both legs from front to back to join together. Place marker for new end of round, then dc20 around each leg to create a 40-st rnd.

Continue to work this 40-st rnd as follows:

Rnds 1-4 dc (4 rnds)

Rnd 5 (dc2tog, dc8) 4 times (36)

Rnd 6 (dc2tog, dc4) 6 times (30)

Rnds 7-8 dc (2 rnds)

Rnd 9 dc5, dc2 into next st, dc3, dc2 into next st, dc10, dc2 into next st, dc3, dc2 into next st, dc5 (34)

Rnds 10-12 dc (3 rnds)

Rnd 13 dc9, dc2 into next st, dc15, dc2 into next st, dc8 (36)

Rnds 14-15 dc (2 rnds)

Rnd 16 dc9, dc2 into next st, dc3, dc2 into next st, dc14, dc2 into next st, dc3, dc2 into next st, dc3 (40)

Rnd 17 dc

Rnd 18 dc8, ch8, miss 8, dc12, ch8, miss 8, dc4 (40)

Rnd 19 dc

Rnd 20 dc6, (dc2tog) 7 times, dc6, (dc2tog) 7 times (26)

Rnd 21 (dc2tog) 13 times (13)

Rnd 22 (dc2tog) 6 times, dc1 (7)

Break yarn, stuff and gather remaining stitches to close.

Front Legs (make two)

Working in Shale

Rejoin and work 16 sts around each hole in sides of body as follows:

Rnds 1-2 dc (2 rnds)

Rnd 3 (dc2tog, dc6) twice (14)

Rnds 4-5 dc (2 rnds)

Rnd 6 (dc2tog, dc5) twice (12)

Rnds 7-12 dc (6 rnds)

Rnd 13 (dc3, dc2 into next st) 3 times (15)

Rnds 14-15 dc (2 rnds)

Rnd 16 (dc3, dc2tog) 3 times (12)

Rnd 17 dc

Rnd 18 (dc2tog, dc4) twice (10)

Rnd 19 dc

Rnd 20 (dc2tog, dc3) twice (8)

Break yarn.

Stuff the legs and sew the two remaining feet into position by sewing around the hole in the foot to the end of the leg. Ensure the small toes are on the outside.

Claws - working in Steel on back feet and Silver on front feet

Sl st into position on the end of each toe, ch4 and sl st 2, htr1 back down chain

Break yarn and repeat on all toes.

Head

Working in Steel

Begin by dc6 into ring

Rnd 1 (dc2 into next st) 6 times (12)

Rnd 2 (dc1, dc2 into next st) 6 times (18)

Rnd 3 (dc2, dc2 into next st) 6 times (24)

Rnd 4 (dc3, dc2 into next st) 6 times (30)

Rnd 5 (dc4, dc2 into next st) 6 times (36)

Rnd 6 (dc5, dc2 into next st) 6 times (42)

Rnd 7 (dc6, dc2 into next st) 6 times (48)

Rnds 8-13 dc (6 rnds)

Rnd 14 (dc6, dc2tog) 6 times (42)

Continue working 2cm (¾in) LOOP STITCH every stitch when instructed

Rnd 15 dc7 with loops, dc7 without loops, dc7 with loops, dc21 without loops

Rnd 16 dc5, dc2tog with loops, dc5, dc2tog without loops, dc5, dc2tog with loops, (dc5, dc2tog) 3 times without loops (36)

Change to Shale

Rnd 17 dc6 with loops, dc7 without loops, dc6 with loops Shale, (dc2tog, dc1) 5 times, dc2tog Steel without loops (30)

Continue without loops

Rnd 18 (dc3, dc2tog) 4 times Silver, (dc3, dc2tog) twice Steel (24)

Continue in Silver

Rnds 19-20 dc (2 rnds)

Rnd 21 (dc2, dc2tog) 6 times (18)

Rnds 22-26 dc (5 rnds)

Rnd 27 (dc2tog) 9 times (9)

Stuff and gather remaining stitches to close.

Ears (make two)

Working in Steel

Begin by dc6 into ring

Rnd 1 (dc1, dc2 into next st) 3 times (9)

Rnd 2 dc

Rnd 3 (dc2, dc2 into next st) 3 times (12)

Rnd 4 (dc3, dc2 into next st) 3 times (15)

Rnd 5 (dc4, dc2 into next st) 3 times (18)

Rnd 6 dc

Rnd 7 (dc5, dc2 into next st) 3 times (21)

Rnds 8-9 dc (2 rnds)

Do not stuff. Sew flat across bottom to close and sew into position on head.

Working in Silver, embroider LONG STITCH in a triangle formation on the inside of each ear.

Tail

Working in Steel

Ch12 and sl st to join into a circle

Work 2.5cm (1in) LOOP STITCH every 2nd st on odd rnds and every 3rd st on even rnds

Rnds 1-3 dc (3 rnds)

Rnd 4 (dc5, dc2 into next) twice (14)

Rnds 5-7 dc (3 rnds)

Rnd 8 (dc6, dc2 into next) twice (16)

Rnds 9-11 dc (3 rnds)

Rnd 12 (dc7, dc2 into next) twice (18)

Rnds 13-15 dc (3 rnds)

Rnd 16 (dc8, dc2 into next) twice (20)

Rnds 17-19 dc (3 rnds)

Rnd 20 (dc9, dc2 into next) twice (22)

Rnds 21-23 dc (3 rnds)

Rnd 24 (dc10, dc2 into next) twice (24)

Change to Silver

Rnds 25-26 dc (2 rnds)

Rnd 27 (dc2, dc2tog) 6 times (18)

Rnd 28 dc

Rnd 29 (dc1, dc2tog) 6 times (12)

Rnd 30 dc

Rnd 31 (dc2tog) 6 times (6)

Break yarn, gather stitches. Do not stuff.

Embroider LONG STITCH in a triangle formation onto the chest in Silver and onto the back of the body in Steel *(see Embroidery)*.

Finish by sewing eyes and nose into place with Black yarn.

Posy of Flowers

TO CREATE THIS ACCESSORY YOU WILL NEED

25g Peony, 25g Lime, 25g Cream

Individual Flower

Stem - working in Lime, ch8 and sl st 7 back down chain, break yarn.

Flower Petals - working in Peony, sl st into end of stem, (ch3 and sl st into end of stem) 5 times, break yarn.

Flower Centre - working in Cream, sl st into centre of flower and MAKE BOBBLE (2), break yarn.

To create a posy, make five flowers and sew together by sewing through the stems approx. 3 sts from the bottom.

“Why don't you enjoy the joy of the woods as you walk Red Riding Hood? The smell of the flowers and the songs of the birds.”

Grandmother's Nightwear

TO CREATE THESE ACCESSORIES YOU WILL NEED

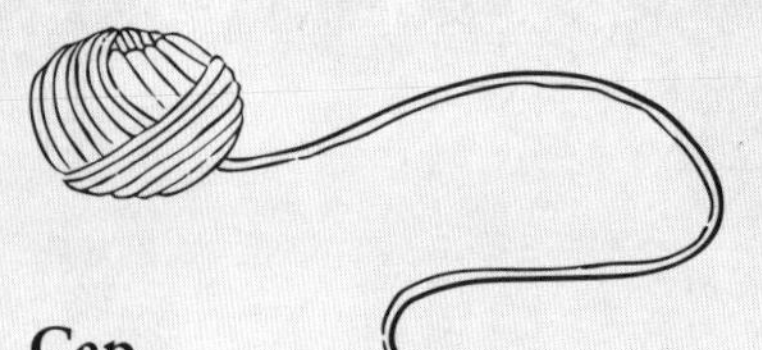

50g Cream, 25g Peony

Doll Glasses

Cap

Working in Peony

Begin by dc6 into ring

Rnd 1 (dc2 into next st) 6 times (12)

Rnd 2 (dc1, dc2 into next st) 6 times (18)

Rnd 3 (dc2, dc2 into next st) 6 times (24)

Rnd 4 (dc3, dc2 into next st) 6 times (30)

Rnd 5 (dc4, dc2 into next st) 6 times (36)

Rnd 6 (dc5, dc2 into next st) 6 times (42)

Rnd 7 (dc6, dc2 into next st) 6 times (48)

Rnd 8 (dc7, dc2 into next st) 6 times (54)

Rnd 9 dc

Rnd 10 (dc8, dc2 into next st) 6 times (60)

Rnds 11-16 dc (6 rnds)

Rnd 17 (dc8, dc2tog) 6 times (54)

Rnd 18 (dc7, dc2tog) 6 times (48)

Rnd 19 (dc6, dc2tog) 6 times (42)

Change to Cream

Rnd 20 htr

Rnd 21 (dc2 into next st, ch3) 42 times

Break yarn.

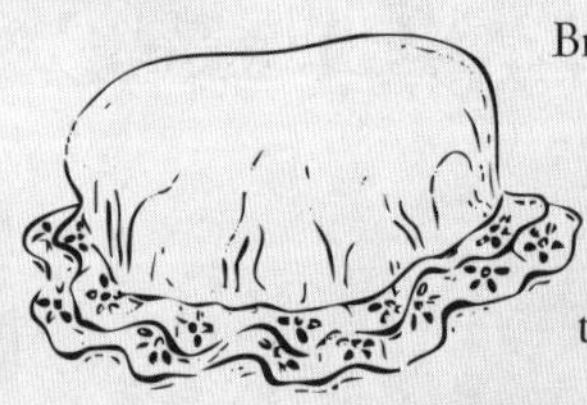

Working in Cream, work a round of sl st around the posts of the htr.

Nightdress

Working in Cream

Ch30 and sl st to join into a circle

Rnd 1 (dc2 into next st) 30 times (60)

Rnds 2-3 dc (2 rnds)

Rnd 4 miss 15 sts for armhole, dc15, miss 15 sts for other armhole, dc15 (30)

Continue to work central 30-st rnd as follows:

Rnd 1 (dc2, dc2 into next st) 10 times (40)

Rnds 2-16 dc (15 rnds)

Rnd 17 (dc3, dc2 into next st) 10 times (50)

Rnds 18-32 dc (15 rnds)

Change to Peony

Rnd 33 (dc2 into next st, ch3) 50 times

Break yarn.

Sleeves - working in Peony, rejoin and work both 15-st armholes as follows:

Rnd 1 (dc2 into next st, ch3) 15 times

Break yarn.

Working in Peony, work a round of dc around the neckline.

Working in Peony, embroider floral design using DAISY STITCH to create the flowers and LONG STITCH for the stems.

CHAPTER TWO

Thumbelina

Once upon a time there was a woman who longed for nothing more than to have a child of her own. So she went to visit an old witch who gave her a piece of magic barley, and told her to plant it in a plant pot and see if her heart's desire could come true.

The very next morning after planting and watering the seed a large single flower grew, much resembling a tightly closed tulip bud. Overawed with wonder at the magic of the flower's growth the woman kissed the beautiful flower, and at once heard a loud crack. The large petals slowly unfolded to reveal it was indeed a real tulip, and at the very centre nestled amongst the stamens sat a very tiny little girl. Beautiful and as small as a fairy, the woman looked at this perfect little child no taller than her thumb-joint and called her Thumbelina.

By day Thumbelina played upon the woman's table as she worked away, dancing and singing with the prettiest little delicate voice you ever did hear. At night she slept under a rose petal blanket inside a walnut shell for a bed. Taking great pleasure in seeing her smile and laugh, one day the woman brought her some tiny round pebbles to play with. As Thumbelina practised throwing them to and fro, one wayward fling smashed a corner at the bottom of the cottage window. Although the woman was not one bit angry about the accident, Thumbelina's apologies could not change the fact that they were unable to afford to replace the broken pane.

Then, one cold dark night, as she lay tucked up and fast asleep, a toad hopped onto the window sill and came in through the broken hole in the glass and thumped down wet and heavy by her bedside.

"What a pretty little wife for my son," the toad declared, and at once took the walnut bed in which the girl was sleeping and leapt from the window back out into the garden with her tucked under her slimy arm. At the bottom of the garden was a wide stream and it was here burrowed in the dank and muddy banks that the toad and her son lived.

"Croak, croak, bleurgh kekex," was all the ugly toad could loudly say as he first laid eyes on the pretty little girl his mother had brought to be his wife.

"Shhhh," hushed his mother, "don't wake her. Let's maroon her on a lily pad where she cannot escape us while we prepare a house here in the mud for you to live once you are wed."

When she awoke, Thumbelina began to cry for she was completely surrounded by water and there was no way for her to make it back to land. Meanwhile the toad was busy preparing a place in the mud for her soon-to-be daughter-in-law, and once she was satisfied the home was ready she swam back to the lily pad with her son. When back at the edge of the lily pad the old toad raised herself above the water and declared, "This is my son, he will be your husband and together you will live happily in your home here in the mud."

"Croak, croak, bleurgh kekex," was all her supposed-betrothed could manage to say as he and his mother swam away again to finish the final preparations for the wedding.

Thumbelina could only cry as the toads swam away, for she had no wish to marry or live with the toad. As her tiny tears dropped into the water lots of little fish popped up their heads to take a look at the tiny girl. Finding her beautiful, they took pity on her and began to gnaw away at the stem of the pad to set her free. Off floated the leaf far away down the stream where the toads could not follow her.

On she sailed, bobbing with the burble of the stream, through the trees filled with birdsong and into a different country. A white butterfly fluttered along with her, the sun shone like gold and everywhere she looked was beautiful. How happy she was now that the toad couldn't get her.

Just then a large beetle came swooping in and with his jagged claws grabbed the tiny girl around her slender waist and flew up into a tree with her. Placing her down upon a leaf he offered her honeydew to eat as he sat and told her just how pretty she looked. Soon the other nosey beetles started to gather around to see her, and quite contrary to her captor's initial thoughts they declared Thumbelina a miserable looking creature who with her two legs and lack of feelers was quite frightful in appearance. Hearing what the other beetles had to say, her admirer became convinced she was in fact ugly after all, and Thumbelina was flown back down to the ground and placed upon a toadstool. There she sat and wept once again, because despite being the prettiest little girl you ever did see, the beetles would have nothing to do with her.

All summer Thumbelina lived alone in the forest, eating the pollen and nectar of flowers, taking shelter in the moss of the forest floor and drinking the morning dew. The leaves of the trees turned to orange and then brown as the nights lengthened and the season changed to the long dark winter. Around her the forest shrivelled in the ice, and it seemed as though she too would die in the frost. Soon snowflakes began to fall, and so shivering with cold she began to wander to the edge of the forest.

Stumbling into a corn field that had been long-since harvested, Thumbelina made her way through the blunt stumps, the icy wind whipping around them. There was not a mouthful of food in sight, when suddenly she came across a mouse's door. Knocking gently at the door with her tiny frozen hands, Thumbelina begged the mouse for a seed of barley, for she had not found anything to eat for days.

"You poor little thing," cried the kindly old mouse, and wrapped Thumbelina up in a cozy warm blanket as she welcomed her in to sit by the fire and share some dinner with her. The field mouse had a tidy house with a well-stocked pantry, and finding herself enjoying the beautiful little girl's company, especially her story-telling, invited her to live with her for the winter.

For Thumbelina time flew by as she kept the little mouse's house clean in the daytime, and spent evenings around the fire sharing tales and singing songs.

One day the mouse declared, "Soon you shall meet my neighbour. His house is much finer than mine and he wears a black velvet coat. If only you could get him for a husband you would be very well provided for, and as his eyesight is not good you must be ready to tell your best stories."

This news was not what Thumbelina wished to hear. The wealthy neighbour was a mole, and she had no desire to marry him, no matter how rich or wise the mouse proclaimed him to be. However, when they met, sing for him she did, and he at once fell in love with her beautiful voice and songs.

The mole had just dug a long passage between his house and that of his friend, so that the mouse and the girl could visit whenever they wished. He warned that on the way back to his house they should pay no attention to a dead bird that had somehow fallen into the tunnel. Sure enough, they soon came across a beautiful swallow, seemingly crash landed into the darkness, huddled up with its head and legs tucked within its wings. Thumbelina at once felt sorry for the bird, thinking of the beautiful birdsong that had kept her company in the forest. Waiting for the others to move on in the tunnel, she bent down and gently kissed the bird on the head, thankful for him and his kind who filled her heart with the happiness of song all summer. Resting her head to the feathers of the bird she heard a very faint beating within his chest. She trembled with surprise and fear, but carefully wrapping some thistledown around the bird for warmth, she stole away into the darkness vowing to return again whenever she next could.

The following night Thumbelina crept out into the tunnel once again, and as she approached, the bird opened one eye only for a moment to look at her. "Thank you," he said, "soon I will be strong enough to fly back into the sunshine." Knowing the swallow was very much too weak to fly anywhere, the girl brought him some water, and once he had drank, told her of how he injured his wing and had no recollection of how he came to be in the dark tunnel underground.

"It's now the winter," Thumbelina told the bird, "and your kin will have all flown away to warmer climes. I will care for you until you are recovered and we can see there are signs of the return of spring."

All winter long the girl cared for her friend the swallow, until one day he pecked back through the hole he had fallen into and golden sunshine bathed them both as they stared up into the blue sky. The swallow asked Thumbelina to go with him, but knowing the old field mouse would be very upset if she were to leave like that, she fondly bid him farewell and watched him fly off over the top of the forest. Her eyes filled with tears for she would miss her friend, and she missed the warm sunshine that she had been forbidden to walk out in.

Returning to the home of the field mouse, Thumbelina was being prepared for her wedding to the mole which was planned for when the sun stopped baking the land hard, and the seasons changed once again into autumn. She worked hard spinning spider silk to make a wedding dress for a wedding she did not want. She did not care at all for the pompous old mole, and instead crept out of the darkness into the light whenever she could to stare up into the sky and wish to see her dear swallow again.

Thumbelina wept as her wedding day grew closer, and the old mouse scolded her for her ingratitude towards having been asked to become the wife of a splendid gentleman with such a well-stocked larder. When the wedding day arrived the girl was waiting to be fetched down into the mole's house deep underground, knowing that never again would she see the sun or feel the wind or smell the scents of summer flowers. Craving one last glimpse of the blue sky she walked but a few steps from the mouse's front door and loudly bid "farewell" to the beauty around her.

Suddenly overhead a loud "tweet" announced the return of her friend the swallow, and he swooped down to wipe away her tears. Hearing she was that very day to be sentenced to be the wife of the mole and forever live in darkness, he at once dropped his shoulder and bid she climb on.

"Today I am flying far away over the forest, mountains and sea to a warmer country where it is always summer, and the flowers are always in bloom. Let me repay you for your kindness in the tunnel for I would have surely frozen to my death without you."

Without hesitation she seated herself on the bird's back and gently held onto his beautiful deep blue feathers as they flew up into the sky, admiring all the beauty of the landscape beneath them. Eventually the chill of the mountains faded away behind them and they flew over warmer countries where the sun beat down brighter than Thumbelina ever knew it could. The air was sweet with scents, the warm winds gently moved through her hair, and beneath them the land was more beautiful than anything she had ever imagined. Finally the swallow swooped down into a field full of tall and beautiful white flowers. To her surprise there in the middle of the flower stood a handsome fairy prince.

Spotting Thumbelina the prince's heart leapt with joy, for she was more lovely than any flower fairy he had ever seen, and at once he asked her if she would like to become his wife and be queen of all the flowers. Finally, here was a husband she could actually love. Not a toad or a mole enforcing her to live in darkness, but a prince with whom she could dance in the sunshine and moonlight for the rest of her life.

All the fairy folk came to rejoice in their love, and to their wedding they brought many beautiful gifts. The greatest and finest of all was a pair of wings, which were strapped to her shoulders so from that day forth and for her happily ever after she could fly up into the sky whenever she wished.

PATTERNS IN THIS STORY

Tulip

Thumbelina

Lily Pad

Toadstools

Swallow

Wedding Outfit & Wings

TO CREATE THE FULL STORY YOU WILL NEED

25g Skin Tone

25g Hair Colour

125g Peony, 125g Cream, 100g Silver, 75g Ruby, 50g Green, 50g Sapphire, 25g Yellow, 25g Lime, 25g Beetroot, 25g Shale

2m (2¼yd) wire

TULIP

TO CREATE THIS SCENERY YOU WILL NEED

125g Peony, 25g Lime, 25g Yellow

2m (2¼yd) wire

Petals (make five)

Working in Peony

Begin by dc6 into ring

Rnd 1 (dc2 into next st) 6 times (12)

Rnd 2 (dc1, dc2 into next st) 6 times (18)

Rnd 3 (dc2, dc2 into next st) 6 times (24)

Rnd 4 (dc3, dc2 into next st) 6 times (30)

Rnd 5 dc

Rnd 6 (dc4, dc2 into next st) 6 times (36)

Rnd 7 dc

Rnd 8 (dc5, dc2 into next st) 6 times (42)

Rnd 9 dc

Rnd 10 (dc13, dc2 into next st) 3 times (45)

Rnds 11-28 dc (18 rnds)

Rnd 29 (dc13, dc2tog) 3 times (42)

Rnd 30 (dc5, dc2tog) 6 times (36)

Rnd 31 dc

Rnd 32 (dc4, dc2tog) 6 times (30)

Rnd 33 dc

Rnd 34 (dc3, dc2tog) 6 times (24)

Rnd 35 dc

Rnd 36 (dc2, dc2tog) 6 times (18)

Rnd 37 (dc1, dc2tog) 6 times (12)

Do not stuff. Gather remaining stitches to close.

Base

Working in Lime

Begin by dc6 into ring

Rnd 1 (dc2 into next st) 6 times (12)

Rnd 2 (dc1, dc2 into next st) 6 times (18)

Rnd 3 (dc2, dc2 into next st) 6 times (24)

Rnd 4 (dc3, dc2 into next st) 6 times (30)

Break yarn.

Sepals

Working in Yellow

Begin by dc6 into ring

Rnd 1 (dc1, MAKE BOBBLE(6) into same st) 6 times (12)

Rnd 2 (dc1, dc2 into next st) 6 times (18)

Rnd 3 (dc2 into next st) 18 times (36)

Rnd 4 (ch6 and sl st 5 back down chain, sl st 2 along main rnd) 18 times

Break yarn.

Sew the petals around the edge of the base. Insert wire into the petals if desired, then sew the sepals into position in centre of flower.

Stem

Working in Lime

Begin by dc6 into ring

Rnd 1 (dc1, dc2 into next st) 3 times (9)

Rnds 2-60 dc (59 rnds)

Rnd 61 (dc2 into next st) 12 times (18)

Rnd 62 (dc2, dc2 into next st) 6 times (24)

Rnd 63 (dc3, dc2 into next st) 6 times (30)

Rnd 64 (ch9 and sl st 1, dc1, htr2, tr2, dtr1, ttr1 back down chain, miss 5, sl st 1 along main rnd) 5 times

Break yarn.

Sew into position by sewing the central circle onto the base at the back of the flower.

Thumbelina

TO CREATE THIS CHARACTER YOU WILL NEED

25g Skin Tone (Camel), 25g Hair Colour (Mushroom), 25g Silver, 25g Yellow, 25g Cream

Body & Head

Working in Yellow

Ch6 and work around chain as follows:

Rnd 1 dc4, dc2 into next st along one side of chain, dc4, dc2 into next st along other side of chain (12)

Rnd 2 (dc2 into next st) 12 times (24)

Rnds 3-8 dc (6 rnds)

Rnd 9 (dc4, dc2tog) 4 times (20)

Rnd 10 dc

Rnd 11 (dc4, dc2 into next st) 4 times (24)

Rnds 12-13 dc (2 rnds)

Change to Skin Tone

Rnds 14-15 dc (2 rnds)

Rnd 16 (dc2tog) 4 times, dc3, (dc2tog) 4 times, dc3, dc2tog (15)

Rnd 17 (dc2tog) 7 times, dc1 (8)

Rnd 18 dc

Rnd 19 dc2, dc3 into next st, dc5 (10)

Rnd 20 dc2 into next st, dc2, (dc2 into next st) 3 times, dc2, dc2 into next st, dc1 (15)

Rnd 21 (dc2 into next st) 15 times (30)

Rnds 22-23 dc (2 rnds)

Rnd 24 dc10, (dc2tog) 4 times, dc12 (26)

Rnds 25-30 dc (6 rnds)

Rnd 31 (dc2tog) 13 times (13)

Rnd 32 (dc2tog) 6 times, dc1 (7)

Stuff and gather remaining stitches to close.

Arms (make two)

Working in Skin Tone

Begin by dc6 into ring

Rnd 1 (dc1, dc2 into next st) 3 times (9)

Rnds 2-5 dc (4 rnds)

Rnd 6 (dc1, dc2tog) 3 times (6)

Rnds 7-11 dc (5 rnds)

Rnd 12 dc2 into next st, dc5 (7)

Rnds 13-14 dc (2 rnds)

Rnd 15 dc2 into next, dc6 (8)

Rnds 16-20 dc (5 rnds)

Stuff hand and sew flat across top to close.

“The large petals slowly unfolded to reveal it was indeed a real tulip, and at the very centre nestled amongst the stamens sat a very tiny little girl.”

Legs (make two)

Working in Skin Tone

Ch9 and work around chain as follows:

Rnd 1 dc7, dc2 into next st along one side of chain, dc7, dc2 into next st along other side of chain (18)

Rnds 2-3 dc (2 rnds)

Rnd 4 (dc2tog) 3 times, dc6, (dc2tog) 3 times (12)

Rnd 5 (dc2tog) twice, dc4, (dc2tog) twice (8)

Rnds 6-8 dc (3 rnds)

Rnd 9 dc2 into next st, dc7 (9)

Rnds 10-12 dc (3 rnds)

Rnd 13 dc2 into next st, dc8 (10)

Rnds 14-15 dc (2 rnds)

Stuff foot and sew flat across top to close.

Sew up your doll *(see Stuffing & Sewing Up)*.

Sew eyes into place with Black yarn and nose with Skin Tone yarn.

Working in Hair Colour use ch12 CHAIN LOOPS between the hairline and the back of the head and then work fifteen ch30 CHAIN LOOPS to create the pony tail *(see Hairstyles)*.

Flowers for Hair (make four)

Working in Cream

Begin by dc5 into ring

Rnd 1 (ch3 and sl st 2 back down chain, sl st 1 along main rnd) 5 times

Break yarn.

Working in Yellow, sl st into flower centre and MAKE BOBBLE(2).

Sew flowers into position around the hair.

Dress

Working in Silver

Ch24 and sl st to join into a circle

Rnds 1-6 dc (6 rnds)

Rnd 7 (dc3, dc2 into next st) 6 times (30)

Turn piece so that you are working in the opposite direction and continue to work in the round as follows:

Rnds 8-9 (ch16 and sl st 15 back down chain, dc3 along main rnd) 10 times (2 rnds)

Rnd 10 (ch16 and sl st 15 back down chain, dc2, dc2 into next st) 10 times (40)

Rnd 11 (ch16 and sl st 15 back down chain, dc3, dc2 into next st) 10 times (50)

Break yarn.

Lily Pad

TO CREATE THIS SCENERY YOU WILL NEED

50g Green

Sides (make two)

Working in Green

Begin by dc6 into ring

Rnd 1 (dc2 into next st) 6 times (12)

Rnd 2 (dc1, dc2 into next st) 6 times (18)

Rnd 3 (dc2, dc2 into next st) 6 times (24)

Rnd 4 (dc3, dc2 into next st) 6 times (30)

Rnd 5 (dc4, dc2 into next st) 6 times (36)

Rnd 6 (dc5, dc2 into next st) 6 times (42)

Rnd 7 (dc6, dc2 into next st) 6 times (48)

Rnd 8 (dc7, dc2 into next st) 6 times (54)

Rnd 9 (dc8, dc2 into next st) 6 times (60)

Rnd 10 (dc9, dc2 into next st) 6 times (66)

Rnd 11 (dc10, dc2 into next st) 6 times (72)

Rnd 12 (dc11, dc2 into next st) 6 times (78)

Break yarn on first piece but not second.

Place the two pieces next to each other with both right sides facing you. Continue to use the live loop on hook but begin crocheting around the other piece first as follows:

Rnd 13 (dc12, dc2 into next st) 5 times, dc13 around first side, (dc12, dc2 into next st) 5 times, dc13 around second side (166)

Continue working this 166-st rnd as follows:

Rnd 14 (dc13, dc2 into next st) 5 times, dc13, (dc13, dc2 into next st) 5 times, dc13 (176)

Rnd 15 (dc14, dc2 into next st) 5 times, dc13, (dc14, dc2 into next st) 5 times, dc13 (186)

Rnd 16 (dc15, dc2 into next st) 5 times, dc12, dc2 into next st, (dc15, dc2 into next st) 5 times, dc12, dc2 into next st (198)

Rnd 17 (dc16, dc2 into next st) 5 times, dc13, dc2 into next st, (dc16, dc2 into next st) 5 times, dc13, dc2 into next st (210)

Rnd 18 (dc17, dc2 into next st) 5 times, dc14, dc2 into next st, (dc17, dc2 into next st) 5 times, dc14, dc2 into next st (222)

Fold in half with right sides facing outwards and work through both sides to join the edge as follows:

Rnd 19 (dc18, dc2 into the next st) 5 times, dc16 (116)

Break yarn.

Toadstools

TO CREATE THIS SCENERY YOU WILL NEED

75g Ruby, 75g Cream

SPORING TOADSTOOL

Stem & Gills

Working in Cream

Begin by dc6 into ring

Rnd 1 (dc2 into next st) 6 times (12)

Rnd 2 (dc1, dc2 into next st) 6 times (18)

Rnd 3 (dc2, dc2 into next st) 6 times (24)

Rnd 4 (dc3, dc2 into next st) 6 times (30)

Rnds 5-6 dc (2 rnds)

Rnd 7 (dc3, dc2tog) 6 times (24)

Rnd 8 (dc6, dc2tog) 3 times (21)

Rnd 9 (dc5, dc2tog) 3 times (18)

Rnd 10 dc

Rnd 11 (dc4, dc2tog) 3 times (15)

Rnds 12-17 dc (6 rnds)

Rnd 18 (dc3, dc2tog) 3 times (12)

Rnds 19-24 dc (6 rnds)

Working into front loop only

Rnd 25 (tr2 into next st) 12 times (24)

Continue working as instructed

Rnd 26 (FPtr2 into next st, BPtr1) 12 times (36)

Rnd 27 (FPtr2, BPtr2 into next st) 12 times (48)

Rnd 28 (Fptr2, BPtr1, BPtr2 into next st) 12 times (60)

Rnd 29 (FPtr2, BPtr2, BPtr2 into next st) 12 times (72)

Rnd 30 dc

Break yarn and stuff the stem.

Pileus

Working in Ruby

Begin by dc6 into ring

Rnd 1 (dc2 into next st) 6 times (12)

Rnd 2 (dc1, dc2 into next st) 6 times (18)

Rnd 3 (dc2, dc2 into next st) 6 times (24)

Rnd 4 (dc3, dc2 into next st) 6 times (30)

Rnd 5 (dc4, dc2 into next st) 6 times (36)

Rnd 6 (dc5, dc2 into next st) 6 times (42)

Rnd 7 (dc6, dc2 into next st) 6 times (48)

Rnd 8 (dc7, dc2 into next st) 6 times (54)

Rnd 9 (dc8, dc2 into next st) 6 times (60)

Rnd 10 (dc9, dc2 into next st) 6 times (66)

Rnd 11 (dc10, dc2 into next st) 6 times (72)

Rnd 12 dc

Join the pileus to the stem/gills with a round of dc from the top down, stuffing before fully closed.

Working in Cream, work a round of dc around the bottom of the stem, approximately 5 rnds out from the centre.

Veil - working in Cream, sl st into position on stem, two rounds down from the gills and then work around the stem as follows:

Rnd 1 tr12

Rnd 2 (dc3 into next st) 12 times (36)

Break yarn.

Spots - working in Cream, work spots onto the pileus by working a variety of MAKE BOBBLE sizes.

CAP TOADSTOOL

Stem & Gills

Working in Cream

Work as Sporing Rnds 1-18 then continue to work as follows:

Rnds 19-22 dc (4 rnds)

Working into front loop only

Rnd 23 (tr2 into next st) 12 times (24)

Continue working as instructed

Rnd 24 (FPtr2 into next st, BPtr1) 12 times (36)

Rnd 25 (FPtr2, BPtr2 into next st) 12 times (48)

Rnd 26 (Fptr2, BPtr1, BPtr2 into next st) 12 times (60)

Rnd 27 dc

Break yarn and stuff the stem.

Pileus

Work Sporing Rnds 1-8

Rnd 9 dc

Rnd 10 (dc8, dc2 into next st) 6 times (60)

Rnds 11-14 dc (4 rnds)

Join the pileus to the stem/gills with a round of dc from the top down, stuffing before fully closed. Then continue as follows:

Rnd 1 (dc2tog, dc4) 10 times (50)

Break yarn.

Working in Cream, work a round of dc around the bottom of the stem, approximately 5 rnds out from the centre.

Veil - working in Cream, sl st into position on stem, one round down from the gills and then work around the stem as follows:

Rnd 1 (htr2 into next st) 12 times (24)

Break yarn.

Spots - working in Cream, work spots onto the pileus by working a variety of MAKE BOBBLE sizes.

BUTTON TOADSTOOL

Stem & Gills

Working in Cream

Work as Sporing Rnds 1-18 then continue to work as follows:

Working into front loop only

Rnd 19 (tr2 into next st) 12 times (24)

Continue working as instructed

Rnd 20 (FPtr2 into next st, BPtr1) 12 times (36)

Rnd 21 (FPtr2, BPtr2 into next st) 12 times (48)

Rnd 22 dc

Break yarn and stuff the stem.

Pileus

Work Sporing Rnds 1-4

Rnd 5 dc

Rnd 6 (dc4, dc2 into next st) 6 times (36)

Rnd 7 dc

Rnd 8 (dc5, dc2 into next st) 6 times (42)

Rnd 9 dc

Rnd 10 (dc6, dc2 into next st) 6 times (48)

Rnd 11 dc

Rnd 12 (dc7, dc2 into next st) 6 times (54)

Rnds 13-18 dc (6 rnds)

Rnd 19 (dc7, dc2tog) 6 times (48)

Rnd 20 dc

Join the pileus to the stem/gills with a round of dc from the top down, stuffing before fully closed.

Working in Cream, work a round of dc around the bottom of the stem, approximately 5 rnds out from the centre.

Spots - working in Cream, work spots onto the pileus by working a variety of MAKE BOBBLE sizes.

Swallow

TO CREATE THIS CHARACTER YOU WILL NEED

50g Sapphire, 25g Beetroot, 25g Cream, 25g Shale

Head & Body

Working in Sapphire

Begin by dc6 into ring

Rnd 1 (dc2 into next st) 6 times (12)

Rnd 2 (dc1, dc2 into next st) 6 times (18)

Rnd 3 (dc2, dc2 into next st) 6 times (24)

Rnd 4 (dc3, dc2 into next st) 6 times (30)

Rnd 5 dc

Rnd 6 (dc4, dc2 into next st) 6 times (36)

Rnds 7-9 dc (3 rnds)

Rnd 10 dc18 Beetroot, dc18 Sapphire

Rnd 11 (dc2tog, dc4) 3 times Beetroot, (dc2tog, dc4) 3 times Sapphire (30)

Rnd 12 (dc2tog, dc3) 3 times Beetroot, dc15 Sapphire (27)

Rnd 13 (dc2tog, dc2) 3 times Beetroot, dc15 Sapphire (24)

Rnd 14 (dc1, dc2tog) 3 times Beetroot, (dc1, dc2tog) 5 times Sapphire (16)

Continue in Sapphire

Rnd 15 dc

Rnd 16 (dc2 into next st) 6 times, (dc4, dc2 into next st) twice (24)

Change to Cream

Rnd 17 dc

Rnd 18 (dc2, dc2 into next st) 8 times (32)

Rnds 19-20 dc (2 rnds)

Rnd 21 (dc7, dc2 into next st) 4 times (36)

Rnds 22-26 dc (5 rnds)

Rnd 27 (dc3, dc2tog) 6 times, dc6 (30)

Rnds 28-30 dc (3 rnds)

Rnd 31 (dc2, dc2tog) 6 times, dc6 (24)

Rnds 32-34 dc (3 rnds)

Rnd 35 (dc1, dc2tog) 6 times, dc6 (18)

Rnd 36 (dc2tog) 6 times, dc6 (12)

Rnd 37 (dc2, dc2tog) 3 times (9)

Rnd 38 (dc1, dc2tog) twice, dc3 (7)

Stuff and gather remaining stitches to close.

Wings

Working in Sapphire

Begin by dc6 into ring

Rnd 1 (dc2 into next st) 6 times (12)

Rnd 2 (dc1, dc2 into next st) 6 times (18)

Rnd 3 (dc2, dc2 into next st) 6 times (24)

Rnd 4 (dc3, dc2 into next st) 6 times (30)

Rnd 5 (dc4, dc2 into next st) 6 times (36)

Rnd 6 (dc5, dc2 into next st) 6 times (42)

Rnd 7 (dc6, dc2 into next st) 6 times (48)

Rnd 8 (dc7, dc2 into next st) 6 times (54)

Rnd 9 (dc8, dc2 into next st) 6 times (60)

Rnd 10 dc

Rnd 11 (dc9, dc2 into next st) 6 times (66)

Rnd 12 dc

Rnd 13 (dc10, dc2 into next st) 6 times (72)

Rnd 14 dc

dc27, then count 27 sts backwards, split and work these sts as follows:

Rnd 1 dc1, dc2tog, dc19, dc2tog, dc1, dc2tog (24)

Rnd 2 dc

Rnd 3 (dc2tog, dc6) 3 times (21)

Rnd 4 dc

Rnd 5 dc2tog, dc17, dc2tog (19)

Rnd 6 dc2tog, dc17 (18)

Rnd 7 (dc2tog, dc4) 3 times (15)

Rnd 8 (dc2tog, dc3) 3 times (12)

Rnd 9 (dc2tog, dc2) 3 times (9)

Rnd 10 dc2tog, dc7 (8)

Break yarn.

Miss 9 sts along main rnd and rejoin

dc27, then count 27 sts backwards, split and work these sts as follows:

Rnd 1 dc1, dc2tog, dc19, dc2tog, dc1, dc2tog (24)

Rnd 2 dc

Rnd 3 (dc2tog, dc6) 3 times (21)

Rnd 4 dc

Rnd 5 dc2tog, dc17, dc2tog (19)

Rnd 6 dc2tog, dc17 (18)

Rnd 7 (dc2tog, dc4) 3 times (15)

Rnd 8 (dc2tog, dc3) 3 times (12)

Rnd 9 (dc2tog, dc2) 3 times (9)

Rnd 10 dc2tog, dc7 (8)

Break yarn.

Tail

Working in Sapphire

Rejoin and work the central 18-st rnd as follows:

Rnds 1-2 dc (2 rnds)

Rnd 3 (dc2, dc2 into next st) 6 times (24)

Rnds 4-5 dc (2 rnds)

dc6, then count 12 sts backwards, split and work these sts as follows:

Rnds 1, 3, 5, 7 dc

Rnd 2 dc2tog, dc10 (11)

Rnd 4 dc2tog, dc9 (10)

Rnd 6 dc2tog, dc8 (9)

Rnd 8 dc2tog, dc7 (8)

Rnds 9-11 dc (3 rnds)

Rnd 12 (dc2, dc2tog) twice (6)

Break yarn.

Rejoin and work the remaining 12-st rnd as follows:

Rnds 1, 3, 5, 7 dc

Rnd 2 dc2tog, dc10 (11)

Rnd 4 dc2tog, dc9 (10)

Rnd 6 dc2tog, dc8 (9)

Rnd 8 dc2tog, dc7 (8)

Rnds 9-11 dc (3 rnds)

Rnd 12 (dc2, dc2tog) twice (6)

Break yarn.

Feet (make two)

Working in Shale

Begin by dc6 into ring

Rnd 1 (dc2 into next st) 6 times (12)

Rnd 2 dc9, ch3, miss 3 (12)

Rnd 3 (dc1, dc2 into next st) 6 times (18)

Split into three rnds of 6 sts with hole central to middle toe and work each as follows:

Rnds 1-3 dc (3 rnds)

Rnd 4 (dc2 into next st, dc2) twice (8)

Rnds 5-6 dc (2 rnds)

Rnd 7 (dc2tog) 4 times (4)

Break yarn.

Legs (make two)

Working in Shale

Rejoin and work 6 sts around the hole in foot (work along the front of the opening first)

Rnds 1-7 dc (7 rnds)

Change to Cream

Rnd 8 (dc1, dc2 into next st) 3 times (9)

Rnd 9 (dc2, dc2 into next st) 3 times (12)

Rnds 10-12 dc (3 rnds)

Break yarn.

Lightly stuff thigh and sew flat across top to close.

Beak

Working in Shale

Ch9 and sl st to join into a circle

Rnds 1-4 dc (4 rnds)

Rnd 5 (dc1, dc2tog) 3 times (6)

Rnd 6 (dc2tog) 3 times (3)

Stuff lightly and sew into position.

Finish by sewing eyes into place with Black yarn.

Wedding Outfit

To create these accessories you will need

75g Cream, 25g Silver

Wedding Dress

Working in Cream

Ch24 and sl st to join into a circle

Rnds 1-8 dc (8 rnds)

Rnd 9 (dc3, dc2 into next st) 6 times (30)

dc10, ch10 then work these 20 sts in the rnd as follows to create a petal:

Rnds 1-2 dc (2 rnds)

Rnd 3 (dc3, dc2tog) 4 times (16)

Rnd 4 dc

Rnd 5 (dc2, dc2tog) 4 times (12)

Rnd 6 (dc1, dc2tog) 4 times (8)

Rnd 7 (dc2, dc2tog) twice (6)

Break yarn.

Rejoin and work two more petals in the same way.

Rejoin and dc10 along the back chain of each petal, then continue to work this 30-st rnd as follows:

Rnds 1-2 dc (2 rnds)

Rnd 3 (dc2, dc2 into next st) 10 times (40)

Rnd 4 dc

Rnd 5 (dc3, dc2 into next st) 10 times (50)

dc10, ch10 then work these 20 sts in the rnd as follows to create a petal:

Rnds 1-2 dc (2 rnds)

Rnd 3 (dc3, dc2tog) 4 times (16)

Rnd 4 dc

Rnd 5 (dc2, dc2tog) 4 times (12)

Rnd 6 (dc1, dc2tog) 4 times (8)

Rnd 7 (dc2, dc2tog) twice (6)

Break yarn.

Rejoin and work four more petals in the same way.

Sew around the underside of the bottom petals to close the chain openings.

Crown

Working in Silver

Ch24 and sl st to join into a circle

Rnd 1 dc

Rnd 2 (dc3, dc2 into next st) 6 times (30)

Change to Cream

Rnds 3-4 dc (2 rnds)

dc10, ch10 then work these 20 sts in the rnd as follows to create a petal:

Rnds 1-2 dc (2 rnds)

Rnd 3 (dc3, dc2tog) 4 times (16)

Rnd 4 dc

Rnd 5 (dc2, dc2tog) 4 times (12)

Rnd 6 (dc1, dc2tog) 4 times (8)

Rnd 7 (dc2, dc2tog) twice (6)

Break yarn.

Rejoin and work two more petals in the same way.

Working in Silver, work a round of sl st around the starting chain. Break yarn and work another round of sl st around the colour change line.

“Spotting Thumbelina the prince's heart leapt with joy.”

Boots (make two)

Working in Silver

Ch9 and work around chain as follows:

Rnd 1 dc7, dc2 into next st along one side of chain, dc7, dc2 into next st along other side of chain (18)

Rnds 2-3 dc (2 rnds)

dc14, then count 10 sts backwards, split and work these sts as follows:

Rnd 1 (dc1, dc2 into next st) 5 times (15)

Rnd 2 dc

Break yarn.

Rejoin and work the remaining 8-st rnd as follows:

Rnd 1 dc2, (dc2tog) twice, dc2 (6)

Rnd 2 dc

Rnd 3 (dc2tog) 3 times (3)

Do not stuff.

WINGS

TO CREATE THIS ACCESSORY YOU WILL NEED

75g Silver, 25g Cream

Wing Panels (make eight)

For full technical diagram see Reading a Pattern

Working in Silver

Ch21 and work around chain as follows:

Rnd 1 sl st 20 along one side of chain, dc20 along other side of chain (40)

Rnd 2 sl st 2, dc2, htr2, tr2, dtr10, tr2, dtr2 into next st, dtr7, tr4, htr4, dc4 (41)

Rnd 3 dc

Break yarn.

Working in Silver, place two wing panels together with right sides facing outwards and join together with a round of dc through both sides around the edge. Repeat for all wing panels to create four wings. (The side with the edging facing you will become the front of the wing.)

Working in Cream, SLIP STITCH TRAVERSE 22 sts along the central line of each wing on the front side.

Sew the narrow ends of the four wings together to join.

Working in Cream, embroider DAISY STITCH on either side of the Cream line, working on the front side of the wings.

Working in Silver, create two straps on the centre back of the wings as follows so that the wings can be worn and removed

Sl st into centre top of wings, ch12 and sl st into bottom of wings, ch12 and sl st into top.

"So from that day forth and for her happily ever after she could fly up into the sky whenever she wished."

CHAPTER THREE

Jack & the Beanstalk

Once upon a time there was a poor boy named Jack who lived with his mother in an old cottage in the countryside. It had been a long time since their field had produced any food, and when they had no way of putting the next meal on their plates that evening, Jack's mother sent him off to market to sell their final hope, their last old white cow.

On the way to market Jack met an unusual looking old pedlar by the side of the dusty road who offered him three magic beans in exchange for the cow. When Jack returned home with the small pouch of beans rather than coins, his mother was so horrifically desperate she scolded him and angrily tossed them out of the window. As he went to bed that night, his empty stomach rumbling with hunger, he glanced out of the window and through it he thought he could see a twisting green stalk almost as tall as him growing from the ground in the shadows beside the cottage.

The following morning he awoke to find that indeed a giant, braided ladder of a beanstalk was growing beside the cottage, wider than he could reach around and taller than he could see, reaching far up and through the clouds. Throwing his rucksack over his shoulder he began to climb up the beanstalk, up and up he went until the cottage was only a speck on the ground far below. When he finally reached the clouds he pulled himself up above them and looked up to see he was standing at the foot of a stone castle. Spotting that the giant door lay ajar, he crept inside fearless of what he might find. All of a sudden a thunderous voices echoed off the stone walls:

"Fee, Fi, Fo, Fum..."

At once Jack leapt inside an open cupboard, and peering through the keyhole he watched a giant stomp into the room and take out bags of gold coins that were set upon the side ready to be counted. Jack waited patiently until night had fallen, and then silently crept out of his hiding place, and taking a bag of coins he quickly snook back through the corridor and down the beanstalk to his mother. At the sight of the giant shiny coins his wearied mother cried with joy, and they both lived happily for months as the beanstalk continued to grow alongside their cottage.

Eventually there came a day when once again the cupboards were bare and so Jack threw his rucksack over his shoulder and began to again scale the beanstalk up into the clouds. Following the same path as before he hid himself back into the cupboard, and after not too long he heard the booming cry of, "Fee, Fi, Fo, Fum..." and he held his breath as the giant came into the room and sat down at the biggest table Jack had ever seen.

Upon the table Jack could see a hen and a harp.

"Lay...Sing..." the giant bellowed, and at once the giant red hen laid a huge shiny golden egg, and the harp turned golden and began to sing the sweetest of tunes. As the harp played its beautiful lullaby the giant began to gently snore, and once certain he was asleep, Jack quietly crept out and clambered up the giant table leg. Tucking the giant golden egg into his rucksack, he walked towards the golden harp and admired its soft magical tune. Planning his escape back down the beanstalk Jack lifted the harp into his arms, but the second he did so the harp stopped singing and cried out:

"Master, Master. Help!'"

The giant awoke at once and roared, "Fee, Fi, Fo, Fum!" and lunged to snatch the harp from Jack.

Faster than the giant, Jack jumped upon the hen's back as it flapped its wings to fly down off the table and she scampered away from the noise and rage of the hollering giant. He managed to steer the hen towards the tip of the beanstalk poking through the clouds, and turned her downwards on the twisted green path back to the cottage. He felt the beanstalk begin to sway as just behind him the giant swung onto the top of the stalk. Clinging onto the harp and encouraging the hen to move as quickly as she could he shouted down to his mother on the ground.

"Fetch my axe, fetch my axe!"

No sooner had his boots touched the ground than he swung the axe deep into the flesh of the beanstalk. Leaves flew and his mother and the hen shrieked as he hacked away at the bottom of the stalk, with the bellowing cry of the giant ringing down upon them from above. As the final swing hit the last stem a roar greater than any you could ever imagine could be heard throughout the land as the beanstalk and with it the giant fell head first from the sky.

Jack and his mother lived happily ever after in their cottage which once again had fields full of crops and cows, as well as a hen that regularly laid golden eggs, and the harp had a new master to whom it could play its magical tunes.

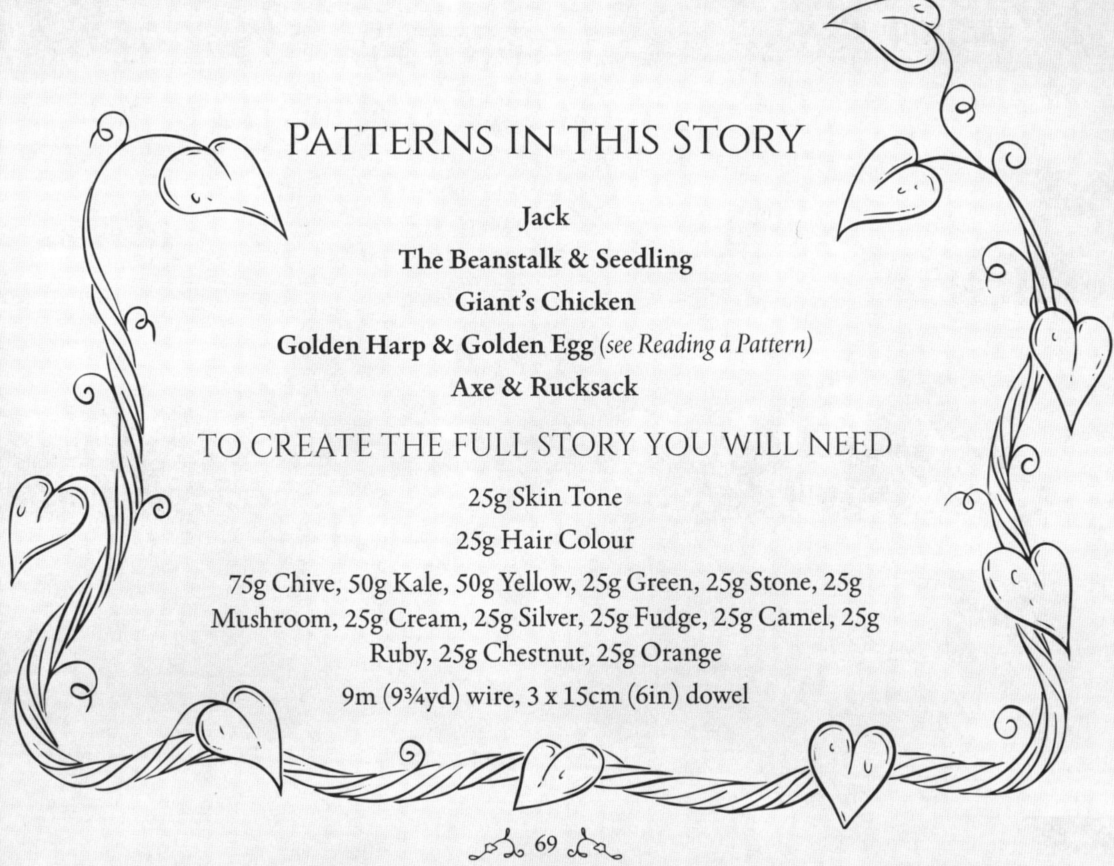

Patterns in this Story

Jack

The Beanstalk & Seedling

Giant's Chicken

Golden Harp & Golden Egg *(see Reading a Pattern)*

Axe & Rucksack

To Create the Full Story You Will Need

25g Skin Tone

25g Hair Colour

75g Chive, 50g Kale, 50g Yellow, 25g Green, 25g Stone, 25g Mushroom, 25g Cream, 25g Silver, 25g Fudge, 25g Camel, 25g Ruby, 25g Chestnut, 25g Orange

9m (9¾yd) wire, 3 x 15cm (6in) dowel

Jack

TO CREATE THIS CHARACTER YOU WILL NEED

25g Skin Tone (Fudge), 25g Hair Colour (Cocoa), 25g Cream, 25g Stone, 25g Mushroom, 25g Ruby

Body & Head

Working in Cream

Ch6 and work around chain as follows:

Rnd 1 dc4, dc2 into next st along one side of chain, dc4, dc2 into next st along other side of chain (12)

Rnd 2 (dc2 into next st) 12 times (24)

Rnds 3-8 dc (6 rnds)

Rnd 9 (dc4, dc2tog) 4 times (20)

Rnd 10 dc

Rnd 11 (dc4, dc2 into next st) 4 times (24)

Rnds 12-15 dc (4 rnds)

Rnd 16 (dc2tog) 4 times, dc3, (dc2tog) 4 times, dc3, dc2tog (15)

Change to Skin Tone

Rnd 17 (dc2tog) 7 times, dc1 (8)

Rnd 18 dc

Rnd 19 dc2, dc3 into next st, dc5 (10)

Rnd 20 dc2 into next st, dc2, (dc2 into next st) 3 times, dc2, dc2 into next st, dc1 (15)

Rnd 21 (dc2 into next st) 15 times (30)

Rnds 22-23 dc (2 rnds)

Rnd 24 dc10, (dc2tog) 4 times, dc12 (26)

Rnds 25-30 dc (6 rnds)

Rnd 31 (dc2tog) 13 times (13)

Rnd 32 (dc2tog) 6 times, dc1 (7)

Stuff and gather remaining stitches to close.

Arms (make two)

Working in Skin Tone

Begin by dc6 into ring

Rnd 1 (dc1, dc2 into next st) 3 times (9)

Rnds 2-5 dc (4 rnds)

Rnd 6 (dc1, dc2tog) 3 times (6)

Rnds 7-11 dc (5 rnds)

Change to Cream

Rnd 12 dc2 into next st, dc5 (7)

Rnds 13-14 dc (2 rnds)

Rnd 15 dc2 into next st, dc6 (8)

Rnds 16-20 dc (5 rnds)

Stuff hand and sew flat across top to close.

Legs (make two)

Working in Skin Tone

Ch9 and work around chain as follows:

Rnd 1 dc7, dc2 into next st along one side of chain, dc7, dc2 into next st along other side of chain (18)

Rnds 2-3 dc (2 rnds)

Rnd 4 (dc2tog) 3 times, dc6, (dc2tog) 3 times (12)

Rnd 5 (dc2tog) twice, dc4, (dc2tog) twice (8)

Rnds 6-8 dc (3 rnds)

Rnd 9 dc2 into next st, dc7 (9)

Rnds 10-12 dc (3 rnds)

Rnd 13 dc2 into next st, dc8 (10)

Rnds 14-15 dc (2 rnds)

Stuff foot and sew flat across top to close.

Sew up your doll (*see Stuffing & Sewing Up*).

Sew eyes into place with Black yarn and nose with Skin Tone yarn.

Working in Hair Colour use SLIP CHAINS, working ch4 across the whole scalp *(see Hairstyles)*.

Cuffs - working in Cream, work a round of htr around the colour change line on each arm.

Collar - work a round of stitches in Cream around the colour change line on neck as follows:

sl st into centre front of neckline, ch2, then tr into each st around the neck

Buttons - working in Stone, embroider four FRENCH KNOTS down the centre front of body to create the buttons.

Shorts

Working in Stone

Ch24 and sl st to join into a circle

Rnd 1 (dc5, dc2 into next st) 4 times (28)

Rnds 2-7 dc (6 rnds)

Split into two rnds of 14 sts and work each as follows:

Rnds 1-2 dc (2 rnds)

Break yarn.

Place shorts onto doll and finish by adding two KNOT LENGTHS to the bottom edge.

Belt

Working in Mushroom

Ch37 and dc36 back down chain

Tie around the waist and sew to secure.

Boots (make two)

Working in Mushroom

Ch9 and work around chain as follows:

Rnd 1 dc7, dc2 into next st along one side of chain, dc7, dc2 into next st along other side of chain (18)

Rnd 2 dc2 into next st, dc15, dc2 into next st, dc1 (20)

Rnds 3-5 dc (3 rnds)

Rnd 6 (dc2tog) 3 times, dc8, (dc2tog) 3 times (14)

Rnd 7 dc2tog, dc10, dc2tog (12)

Break yarn.

Hat

Working in Stone

Begin by dc6 into ring

Rnd 1 (dc2 into next st) 6 times (12)

Rnd 2 (dc1, dc2 into next st) 6 times (18)

Rnd 3 dc

Rnd 4 (dc2 into next st) 3 times, dc15 (21)

Rnd 5 (dc1, dc2 into next st) 3 times, dc15 (24)

Rnd 6 dc4, dc2 into next st, dc19 (25)

Rnd 7 dc5, dc2 into next st, dc19 (26)

Rnd 8 dc6, dc2 into next st, dc19 (27)

Rnd 9 dc7, dc2 into next st, dc19 (28)

Rnd 10 dc8, dc2 into next st, dc19 (29)

Rnd 11 dc9, dc2 into next st, dc19 (30)

Turn piece so that you are working in the opposite direction and continue to work in the round as follows:

Rnd 12 (dc4, dc2 into next st) 6 times (36)

Rnd 13 (dc11, dc2 into next st) 3 times (39)

Change to Mushroom

Rnd 14 sl st

Break yarn.

Fold the bottom edge of the hat upwards, pinch the front of the brim into a point and sew to secure (the line of increasing is the front of the hat).

Feather - working in Ruby

Sl st into side of hat, ch8 and sl st 2, dc2, sl st 3 back down chain

Beanstalk Seedling

TO CREATE THIS SCENERY YOU WILL NEED

25g Chive

1m (1yd) Wire

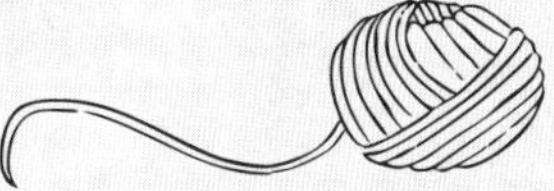

Vine

Working in Chive

Begin by dc6 into ring

Working into back loop only

Rnd 1 dc

Continue working through whole stitch

Rnds 2-15 dc (14 rnds)

Rnd 16 dc2tog, dc4 (5)

Rnds 17-26 dc (10 rnds)

Rnd 27 dc2tog, dc3 (4)

Rnds 28-30 dc (3 rnds)

Break yarn. Do not stuff.

Insert wire and twist into shape.

Make leaves as desired from the following patterns and then add to the vine by working the stem.

Small Leaf

Ch2 and work all stitches into the 2nd chain from hook

tr3, htr3, tr1, htr3, tr3, ch2 and sl st into central chain

Break yarn and pull end tight to close the hole.

Large Leaf

Ch3 and work all stitches into the 3rd chain from hook

dtr3, tr3, dtr1, tr3, dtr3, ch2 and sl st into central chain

Break yarn and pull end tight to close the hole.

Stem

Sl st into leaf, ch3 and sl st into vine, then sl st back along chain. Break yarn.

Cut a 15cm (6in) length of wire and insert into the vine.

"He thought he could see a twisting green stalk almost as tall as him growing from the ground in the shadows beside the cottage."

The Beanstalk

TO CREATE THIS SCENERY YOU WILL NEED

75g Chive, 50g Kale, 25g Green

8m (8¾yd) Wire

NOTE: stuff as you go along, but if using wire this can be added once complete.

Small Vine (make three)

Working in Chive

Begin by dc6 into ring

Rnd 1 (dc2 into next st) 6 times (12)

Working into back loop only

Rnd 2 dc

Continue working through whole stitch

Rnds 3-10 dc (8 rnds)

Rnd 11 dc2tog, dc10 (11)

Rnds 12-19 dc (8 rnds)

Rnd 20 dc2tog, dc9 (10)

Rnds 21-30 dc (10 rnds)

Rnd 31 dc2tog, dc8 (9)

Rnds 32-43 dc (12 rnds)

Rnd 44 dc2tog, dc7 (8)

Rnds 45-56 dc (12 rnds)

Rnd 57 dc2tog, dc6 (7)

Rnds 58-71 dc (14 rnds)

Rnd 72 dc2tog, dc5 (6)

Rnds 73-86 dc (14 rnds)

Rnd 87 dc2tog, dc4 (5)

Rnds 88-101 dc (14 rnds)

Rnd 102 dc2tog, dc3 (4)

Rnds 103-108 dc (6 rnds)

Break yarn.

Medium Vine (make one in Chive and one in Green)

Begin by dc6 into ring

Rnd 1 (dc2 into next st) 6 times (12)

Rnd 2 (dc1, dc2 into next st) 6 times (18)

Working into back loop only

Rnd 3 dc

Continue working through whole stitch

Rnds 4-11 dc (8 rnds)

Rnd 12 (dc2tog, dc1) twice, dc12 (16)

Rnds 13-20 dc (8 rnds)

Rnd 21 dc10, (dc2tog, dc1) twice (14)

Rnds 22-29 dc (8 rnds)

Rnd 30 (dc1, dc2tog) twice, dc8 (12)

Rnds 31-40 dc (10 rnds)

Rnd 41 dc2tog, dc10 (11)

Rnds 42-51 dc (10 rnds)

Rnd 52 dc2tog, dc9 (10)

Rnds 53-62 dc (10 rnds)

Rnd 63 dc2tog, dc8 (9)

Rnds 64-73 dc (10 rnds)

Rnd 74 dc2tog, dc7 (8)

Rnds 75-84 dc (10 rnds)

Rnd 85 dc2tog, dc6 (7)

Rnds 86-91 dc (6 rnds)

Rnd 92 dc2tog, dc5 (6)

Rnds 93-98 dc (6 rnds)

Rnd 99 dc2tog, dc4 (5)

Rnds 100-105 dc (6 rnds)

Rnd 106 dc2tog, dc3 (4)

Break yarn.

Large Vine

Working in Kale

Begin by dc6 into ring

Rnd 1 (dc2 into next st) 6 times (12)

Rnd 2 (dc1, dc2 into next st) 6 times (18)

Rnd 3 (dc2, dc2 into next st) 6 times (24)

Working into back loop only

Rnd 4 dc

Continue working through whole stitch

Rnds 5-12 dc (8 rnds)

Rnd 13 (dc2tog, dc1) twice, dc18 (22)

Rnds 14-21 dc (8 rnds)

Rnd 22 dc16, (dc2tog, dc1) twice (20)

Rnds 23-30 dc (8 rnds)

Rnd 31 (dc1, dc2tog) twice, dc14 (18)

Rnds 32-41 dc (10 rnds)

Rnd 42 dc2tog, dc16 (17)

Rnds 43-52 dc (10 rnds)

Rnd 53 dc2tog, dc15 (16)

Rnds 54-63 dc (10 rnds)

Rnd 64 dc2tog, dc14 (15)

Rnds 65-74 dc (10 rnds)

Rnd 75 dc2tog, dc13 (14)

Rnds 76-81 dc (6 rnds)

Rnd 82 dc2tog, dc12 (13)

Rnds 83-88 dc (6 rnds)

Rnd 89 dc2tog, 11 (12)

Rnds 90-93 dc (4 rnds)

Rnd 94 dc2tog, dc10 (11)

Rnds 95-98 dc (4 rnds)

Rnd 99 dc2tog, dc9 (10)

Rnds 100-103 dc (4 rnds)

Rnd 104 dc2tog, dc8 (9)

Rnds 105-108 dc (4 rnds)

Rnd 109 dc2tog, dc7 (8)

Rnds 110-113 dc (4 rnds)

Rnd 114 dc2tog, dc6 (7)

Rnds 115-116 dc (2 rnds)

Rnd 117 dc2tog, dc5 (6)

Break yarn.

Insert wire into the vines and twist together to make the beanstalk stand. Alternatively, if not using wire, stuff and sew the vines into place twisting around each other.

Leaves - working in Chive, make leaves as for the **Beanstalk Seedling** as desired and then add to the Chive vines.

"Throwing his rucksack over his shoulder he began to climb up the beanstalk."

Giant's Chicken

TO CREATE THIS CHARACTER YOU WILL NEED

25g Chestnut, 25g Fudge, 25g Yellow, 25g Ruby,
25g Camel, 25g Orange

Centraliser

Body, Neck & Head

Working in Chestnut

Begin by dc6 into ring

Rnd 1 (dc2 into next st) 6 times (12)

Rnd 2 (dc1, dc2 into next st) 6 times (18)

Rnd 3 (dc2, dc2 into next st) 6 times (24)

Rnd 4 (dc3, dc2 into next st) 6 times (30)

Rnd 5 (dc4, dc2 into next st) 6 times (36)

Rnd 6 (dc5, dc2 into next st) 6 times (42)

Rnd 7 (dc6, dc2 into next st) 6 times (48)

Rnd 8 (dc7, dc2 into next st) 6 times (54)

Rnd 9 (dc8, dc2 into next st) 6 times (60)

Rnd 10 (dc2, dc1 SPIKE STITCH three rnds below) 20 times (60)

Rnds 11-12 dc (2 rnds)

Change to Fudge

Rnds 13-19 dc (7 rnds)

Rnd 20 dc18, place centraliser, dc24 (incomplete rnd)

Split the 24 stitches marked with your centraliser into the round and work this 24-st round as follows:

Rnds 21-23 dc (3 rnds)

Rnd 24 (dc6, dc2tog) 3 times (21)

Rnd 25 (dc5, dc2tog) 3 times (18)

Rnd 26 (dc4, dc2tog) 3 times (15)

Rnd 27 dc

Rnd 28 (dc2 into next st) 15 times (30)

Rnds 29-35 dc (7 rnds)

Rnd 36 (dc3, dc2tog) 6 times (24)

Rnd 37 dc

Rnd 38 (dc2, dc2tog) 6 times (18)

Rnd 39 (dc2tog) 9 times (9)

Gather remaining stitches to close.

Stuff the body, neck and head and then fold the back opening flat and sew across to close.

Beak Base

Working in Ruby

Begin by dc6 into ring

Rnd 1 (dc2 into next st) 6 times (12)

Rnd 2 (dc1, dc2 into next st) 6 times (18)

Sew into position on centre front of head.

Eye Patches (make two)

Working in Ruby

Begin by dc6 into ring

Rnd 1 (dc1, dc2 into next st) 3 times (9)

Sew into position on either side of beak base.

Beak

Working in Yellow

Ch9 and sl st to join into a circle

Rnds 1-2 dc (2 rnds)

Rnd 3 (dc1, dc2tog) 3 times (6)

Rnd 4 dc

Rnd 5 (dc1, dc2tog) twice (4)

Do not stuff. Sew into position on top of beak base.

Wattle (make two)

Working in Ruby

Begin by dc6 into ring

Rnd 1 (dc2 into next st) 6 times (12)

Rnds 2-3 dc (2 rnds)

Rnd 4 (dc2, dc2tog) 3 times (9)

Rnd 5 (dc1, dc2tog) 3 times (6)

Rnd 6 dc

Rnd 7 (dc1, dc2 into next st) 3 times (9)

Do not stuff. Sew into position beneath beak base.

Comb

Working in Ruby

Ch32 and sl st to join into a circle

dc8, split and work these 8 sts as follows:

Rnd 1 (dc1, dc2 into next st) 4 times (12)

Rnds 2-3 dc (2 rnds)

Rnd 4 (dc2, dc2tog) 3 times (9)

Rnd 5 (dc1, dc2tog) 3 times (6)

Rnd 6 (dc2tog) 3 times (3)

Break yarn.

Rejoin and work the remaining 24-st rnd as follows:

Rnd 1 dc

Split into three rnds of 8 sts and work the first 8-st rnd as follows:

Rnd 1 dc

Rnd 2 (dc1, dc2 into next st) 4 times (12)

Rnd 3 dc

Rnd 4 (dc2, dc2tog) 3 times (9)

Rnd 5 (dc1, dc2tog) 3 times (6)

Rnd 6 (dc2tog) 3 times (3)

Break yarn.

Work the next 8-st rnd as follows:

Rnds 1-2 dc (2 rnds)

Rnd 3 (dc2, dc2tog) twice (6)

Rnd 4 (dc1, dc2tog) twice (4)

Break yarn.

Work the next 8-st rnd as follows:

Rnd 1 (dc2, dc2tog) twice (6)

Rnd 2 (dc1, dc2tog) twice (4)

Break yarn.

Stuff the back large spike lightly and sew into position on top of head.

Feet (make two)

Working in Yellow

Begin by dc6 into ring

Rnd 1 (dc2 into next st) 6 times (12)

Rnd 2 (dc3, dc2 into next st) 3 times (15)

Rnd 3 ch4, miss 4, dc2, (dc2, dc2 into next st) 3 times (18)

Rnd 4 dc

Split into three rnds of 6 sts and work each as follows:

Rnds 1-9 dc (9 rnds)

Rnd 10 (dc2tog) 3 times (3)

Break yarn.

Legs (make two)

Working in Yellow

Rejoin and work 8 sts around the hole in foot (work along the front of the opening first)

Rnds 1-3 dc (3 rnds)

Rnd 4 (dc1, dc2 into next st) 4 times (12)

Rnds 5-6 dc (2 rnds)

Rnd 7 (dc1, dc2tog) 4 times (8)

Rnds 8-10 dc (3 rnds)

Change to Chestnut

Rnd 11 (dc1, dc2 into next st) 4 times (12)

Rnds 12-15 dc (4 rnds)

Break yarn.

Lightly stuff feet and thighs and sew legs into position on bottom of body.

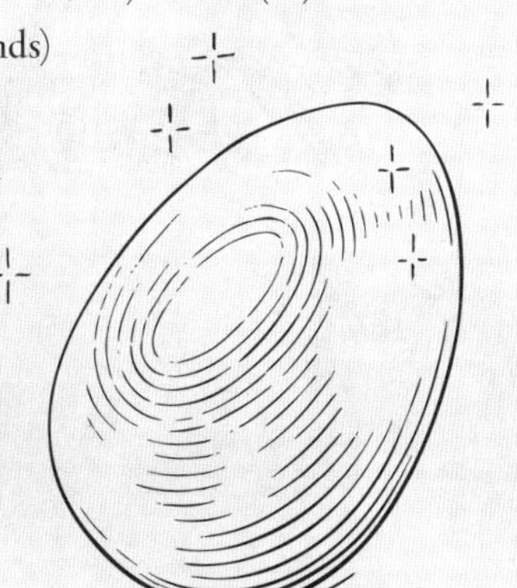

Feathers (make one in Fudge, one in Camel and one in Chestnut)

Ch18 and miss 2, htr5, tr11 back down chain

Ch15 and miss 2, htr5, tr8 back down chain

Ch13 and miss 2, htr5, tr6 back down chain

Ch13 and miss 2, htr5, tr6 back down chain

Ch15 and miss 2, htr5, tr8 back down chain

Ch18 and miss 2, htr5, tr11 back down chain

Break yarn.

Sew the Chestnut row of feathers into position on the back end of the body. Line the centre of the feathers up with the tail end of the central seam and sew either end to meet the colour change line below.

Sew the row of Camel feathers in front of this, followed by the Fudge feathers.

Working in Orange

Work two more feathers between the Chestnut and Camel rows as follows:

sl st into central line of body, ch15 and miss 2, htr5, tr8 back down chain, sl st into body, then turn and work a second feather in the same way behind the first.

Golden Harp

TO CREATE THIS ACCESSORY YOU WILL NEED

25g Yellow, 25g Silver

2 x 15cm (6in) Dowel

Soundbox (diagonal)

Working in Yellow

Begin by dc6 into ring

Rnds 1-20 dc (20 rnds)

Break yarn.

Pillar (vertical)

Working in Yellow

Begin by dc6 into ring

Rnds 1-21 dc (21 rnds)

Rnd 22 (dc2 into next st) 6 times (12)

Rnd 23 (dc3, dc2 into next st) 3 times (15)

Rnd 24 (dc4, dc2 into next st) 3 times (18)

Rnd 25 (dc2, dc2 into next st) 6 times (24)

Break yarn.

Base

Working in Yellow

Begin by dc6 into ring

Rnd 1 (dc2 into next st) 6 times (12)

Rnd 2 (dc1, dc2 into next st) 6 times (18)

Rnd 3 (dc2, dc2 into next st) 6 times (24)

Do not break yarn. Insert dowels and sew open end of soundbox onto wide bottom of the pillar. Attach base to bottom of pillar with DC JOIN.

Neck

Working in Yellow

Sl st into position 3 rnds down from top of soundbox, ch16 and sl st into pillar 3 rnds down from top. Sl st 1 down pillar, then htr16 back along chain and sl st into soundbox. Break yarn.

Strings

Working in Silver, sew between base and neck twisting yarn around the string on the return.

Axe & Rucksack

TO CREATE THESE ACCESSORIES YOU WILL NEED

25g Mushroom, 25g Cocoa, 25g Silver, Length of Stone

1 x 15cm (6in) Dowel

Axe Handle

Working in Cocoa

Begin by dc6 into ring

Rnds 1-22 dc (22 rnds)

Break yarn. Insert dowel and gather stitches to close.

Axe Blade

Working in Silver

Begin by dc6 into ring

Rnd 1 (dc1, dc2 into next st) 3 times (9)

Rnd 2 dc2 into next st, dc1, ch2, miss 2, dc3, ch2, miss 2 (10)

Rnd 3 (dc4, dc2 into next st) twice (12)

Rnd 4 (dc5, dc2 into next st) twice (14)

Rnd 5 (dc6, dc2 into next st) twice (16)

Fold flat and dc through both sides to close.

Push the handle through the chain hole on blade.

Rucksack

See Giant's Chicken for image

Working in Mushroom

Begin by dc6 into ring

Rnd 1 (dc2 into next st) 6 times (12)

Rnd 2 (dc1, dc2 into next st) 6 times (18)

Rnd 3 (dc2, dc2 into next st) 6 times (24)

Rnd 4 (dc3, dc2 into next st) 6 times (30)

Working into back loop only

Rnd 5 htr

Continue working through whole stitch

Rnd 6 htr

Rnd 7 (htr2tog, htr8) 3 times (27)

Rnd 8 htr

Rnd 9 (htr2tog, htr7) 3 times (24)

Rnd 10 (htr2tog, htr6) 3 times (21)

Rnd 11 htr

Rnd 12 (dc5, dc2tog) 3 times (18)

Continue to work the next 9 sts in rows as follows:

Row 1 (RS) dc9, turn

Row 2 (WS) dc9, turn

Row 3 (RS) dc9

Break yarn.

Sew the corners of the flap down onto the top edge of the bag, but leaving the bag open so that the Golden Egg *(see Reading a Pattern)* can fit inside.

Working in Stone, embroider stitches onto the front of the rucksack.

Straps (make two)

Sl st into back top corner of rucksack, ch13 and sl st into bottom corner, then sl st back along chain.

> "Jack and his mother lived happily ever after in their cottage which once again had fields full of crops and cows."

CHAPTER FOUR

SNOW WHITE

There was once a queen who pricked her finger as she sat at a window watching snowflakes fall in the middle of winter. As three drops of blood fell in the snow she wished to one day have a daughter. Not long after the queen bore a baby girl, and although she herself died, her daughter lived and the young princess became known to all as 'Snow White'.

After a few years the king found a new wife, a vain and cruel woman who was wise in the ways of witchcraft. Each morning the new queen would stare into her magic mirror and ask:

"Mirror, mirror on the wall, who is the fairest of them all?"

Each day the mirror would reply that she was indeed the most beautiful in the kingdom. Every day, until one day as Snow White turned seven, the mirror replied that the fairness of the young princess had surpassed her own. Envious and enraged she turned against Snow White, her hatred growing towards her step-child until one day, overcome with envy, she orders a huntsman to take her deep into the forest and end her life. The huntsman takes the young girl into the forest, but after raising his dagger, he finds himself unable to kill her. Realising her step-mother's plot Snow White begs the huntsman for her life, promising to never again return to her kingdom. Confident in all the natural dangers of the forest and with his heart full of pity, the huntsman agreed to turn his back as she ran away deeper into the trees towards the mountains.

After hours of wandering through brambles and clambering over moss-covered fallen trees, Snow White stumbled upon a small cottage. Finding no one at home, Snow White gently pushed open the door to discover a table beautifully set with seven bowls, seven forks and seven knives, all with cups set to the side of each setting filled with wine. At once feeling her hunger she took a nibble from a few plates, sips from a few cups, and collapsed into one of the seven perfectly made-up little beds. Finding it comfortable she fell into a deep sleep, and didn't even stir when seven pairs of booted and weary feet trampled through the cottage door. Before they had even hung up their hats the dwarves knew that someone had been inside their cottage, eating their food and drinking their wine. Finally discovering her, but not wanting to wake the beautiful young girl, they left her sleeping and it was only in the morning that Snow White explained how she had come to be in one of their beds. She asked them for sanctuary and the kindly dwarves took pity on her and said that if she could cook and clean for them all then she could live with them in their cottage, sternly warning her that when they headed out to work in the mountains each day she must make sure to never let anyone in.

One day the wicked queen thought to herself how beautiful she looked and so once again turned to her mirror to seek affirmance. Upon hearing that Snow White was alive and living in the forest and was still the fairest of them all, the queen shook with anger. At once she disguised herself and travelled alone to the little cottage to complete the task the huntsman had failed. Knocking upon the door she did almost gasp when she saw the girl's beauty, and offering a basket of wares she tricked her way inside with the promise of a new ribbon. While lacing her dress the queen pulled the straps with all her might, tying them so tight that Snow White fell to the floor as the queen quickly fled the cottage. Thankfully it was not long before the dwarves returned from the mountain, and upon finding her on the floor they quickly cut the ribbon and Snow White took a deep breath. The next day, having reminded her of the very grave danger her step-mother posed, the dwarves marched away to work.

A few days later another check in the mirror revealed to the queen that Snow White still lived, and once again she went in disguise to knock on the cottage door. Just as before the dwarves were out on the mountain, and the queen managed to trick her way through the door with an offer to comb her hair. With intent fuelled by her jealousy she thrust a poison-laced comb into Snow White's scalp and she fell to the floor instantly. When the dwarves returned they were once again horrified to find the girl harmed in their absence, and quickly discovering the source removed the comb from her head. Within moments Snow White's eyes began to blink, and she returned to them .

Standing afore her mirror once again, the queen smirked as she began her question, only to scream in horror as its reply revealed her step daughter still lived. Using the darkest of spells she immediately made herself unrecognisable once again and headed back to the cottage. This time mistrusting of the knock at the door, Snow White refused to allow the old woman inside the cottage. Initially rejecting the offer of the sweetest apples in the land, Snow White is persuaded to take a bite once the old lady offers to cut it in half for them both to share. As the piece of the poisoned side of the apple passed her lips, it seemed the queen was finally triumphant as the girl fell down into a death-like sleep. Unable to revive her the dwarves assumed that this time her step-mother had indeed killed her, and Snow White's body was placed inside a glass casket and they said a sorrowful goodbye to their beautiful princess.

Sometime later a prince stumbles across a glass casket containing a beautiful young woman at the bottom of a mountain. Hearing the story from the dwarves the prince vows to return her to her father's castle and with his men at once lifts her casket and begins the journey. As she is carried through woods and over rocks the casket lurches and the poisoned piece of apple flies free of Snow White's throat. Overjoyed to see the lifeless beautiful princess smile, the prince professes his love to her and they go on to live happily ever after.

Patterns in this Story

Snow White

Pickaxe

Seven Dwarves

Poisioned Apple

Roses

To Create the Full Story You Will Need

25g Skin Tone, 25g Hair Colour, 7 x 50g Skin Tone, 7 x 25g Hair Colour

100g Kale, 75g Chive, 75g Sapphire, 75g Cream, 50g Green, 50g Ruby, 50g Sage, 25 Cocoa, 25g Mushroom, 25g Charcoal, 25g Stone, 25g Chestnut, 25g Fudge, 25g Silver

1 x 15cm (6in) dowel

Snow White

TO CREATE THIS CHARACTER YOU WILL NEED

25g Skin Tone (Oatmeal), 25g Hair Colour (Black), 25g Cream, 25g Sapphire, 25g Ruby

Body & Head

Working in Sapphire

Ch6 and work around chain as follows:

Rnd 1 dc4, dc2 into next st along one side of chain, dc4, dc2 into next st along other side of chain (12)

Rnd 2 (dc2 into next st) 12 times (24)

Rnds 3-8 dc (6 rnds)

Change to Cream

Rnd 9 (dc4, dc2tog) 4 times (20)

Rnd 10 dc

Rnd 11 (dc4, dc2 into next st) 4 times (24)

Rnds 12-15 dc (4 rnds)

Rnd 16 (dc2tog) 4 times, dc3, (dc2tog) 4 times, dc3, dc2tog (15)

Rnd 17 (dc2tog) 7 times, dc1 (8)

Change to Skin Tone

Rnd 18 dc

Rnd 19 dc2, dc3 into next st, dc5 (10)

Rnd 20 dc2 into next st, dc2, (dc2 into next st) 3 times, dc2, dc2 into next st, dc1 (15)

Rnd 21 (dc2 into next st) 15 times (30)

Rnds 22-23 dc (2 rnds)

Rnd 24 dc10, (dc2tog) 4 times, dc12 (26)

Rnds 25-30 dc (6 rnds)

Rnd 31 (dc2tog) 13 times (13)

Rnd 32 (dc2tog) 6 times, dc1 (7)

Stuff and gather remaining stitches to close.

Arms (make two)

Working in Skin Tone

Begin by dc6 into ring

Rnd 1 (dc1, dc2 into next st) 3 times (9)

Rnds 2-5 dc (4 rnds)

Rnd 6 (dc1, dc2tog) 3 times (6)

Change to Cream

Rnds 7-11 dc (5 rnds)

Rnd 12 dc2 into next st, dc5 (7)

Rnds 13-14 dc (2 rnds)

Rnd 15 dc2 into next st, dc6 (8)

Rnds 16-17 dc (2 rnds)

Rnd 18 dc4, (dc2 into next st) 4 times (12)

Rnd 19 dc4, (dc1, dc2 into next st) 4 times (16)

Rnd 20 dc4, (dc3tog) 4 times (8)

Stuff hand and sew flat across top to close.

Legs (make two)

Working in Skin Tone

Ch9 and work around chain as follows:

Rnd 1 dc7, dc2 into next st along one side of chain, dc7, dc2 into next st along other side of chain (18)

Rnds 2-3 dc (2 rnds)

Rnd 4 (dc2tog) 3 times, dc6, (dc2tog) 3 times (12)

Rnd 5 (dc2tog) twice, dc4, (dc2tog) twice (8)

Rnds 6-8 dc (3 rnds)

Rnd 9 dc2 into next st, dc7 (9)

Rnds 10-12 dc (3 rnds)

Rnd 13 dc2 into next st, dc8 (10)

Rnd 14 dc

Change to Sapphire

Rnd 15 dc

Stuff foot and sew flat across top to close.

Sew up your doll *(see Stuffing & Sewing Up)*.

Sew eyes into place with Black yarn and nose with Skin Tone yarn.

Working in Hair Colour use 30cm (12in) KNOT LENGTHS then gather strands from the front, plait and tie to secure *(see Hairstyles)*.

Sleeve Cuffs - working in Cream, tr2 into each st around the colour change line on each arm.

Bloomers - working in Cream, work a round of stitches around the colour change line on each leg as follows:

(ch3, sl st 1) 10 times, break yarn.

Skirt

Working in Sapphire

Ch20 and sl to to join into a circle

Rnd 1 dc

Rnd 2 (dc4, dc2 into next st) 4 times (24)

Rnd 3 dc

Rnd 4 (dc3, dc2 into next st) 6 times (30)

Rnds 5-12 dc (8 rnds)

Change to Cream

Rnd 13 dc

Rnd 14 (dc2 Cream, dc1 Ruby) 10 times

Change to Cream

Rnd 15 dc

Change to Sapphire

Rnds 16-17 dc (2 rnds)

Break yarn.

Working in Cream, fold the bottom of the skirt upwards and work a round of tr2 into each st into the underside of the skirt around the Cream stitches.

Place skirt onto doll and sew into position to secure.

Belt

Working in Ruby

Ch21 and sl st to join into a circle

Rnd 1 dc

Break yarn and sew around waist.

Bodice

Working in Sapphire

Ch16 and work in rows as follows using INVISIBLE ROWS technique on wrong side rows if desired:

Row 1 (RS) dc15, turn

Row 2 (WS) (INV) dc15, turn

Row 3 (RS) dc15, turn

Row 4 (WS) (INV) dc15, turn

Row 5 (RS) dc15

Break yarn and sew into position on body, leaving a gap at the back for the lacing.

Lacing - working in Ruby, work ch6 laces in a cross formation, sl st into the edge of the bodice between each ch6.

Headband

Working in Cream

Ch28 and sl st to join into a circle

Rnd 1 dc

Break yarn and sew into position on head.

Cloak

Working in Ruby

Ch31 and sl st back down chain, break yarn.

Working in Sapphire

Missing 9 sts from the end, rejoin onto the Ruby chain and work the central 12 sts in rows as follows, using INVISIBLE ROWS technique on wrong side rows if desired:

Row 1 (RS) dc12

Rows 2, 4, 6 (WS) (INV) dc

Row 3 (RS) (dc1, dc2 into next st) 6 times (18)

Row 5 (RS) (dc2 into next st, dc2) 6 times (24)

Rows 7-15 dc continuing INVISIBLE ROWS technique on wrong side rows (9 rows)

Change to Cream

Row 16 (WS) (INV) dc

Row 17 (RS) dc1 Cream, dc1 Ruby, (dc2 Cream, dc1 Ruby) 7 times, dc1 Cream

Continue in Cream

Row 18 (WS) (INV) dc

Change to Sapphire

Row 19 dc

Break yarn.

Working in Cream, work two rows of dc along each side edge, using INVISIBLE ROWS technique on wrong side rows if desired. Then work tr2 into each stitch along the top edge.

Shoes (make two)

Working in Black

Ch9 and work around chain as follows:

Rnd 1 dc7, dc2 into next st along one side of chain, dc7, dc2 into next st along other side of chain (18)

Rnd 2 dc2 into next st, dc15, dc2 into next st, dc1 (20)

Rnds 3-5 dc (3 rnds)

Rnd 6 (dc2tog) 3 times, dc8, (dc2tog) 3 times (14)

Break yarn.

Pickaxe

TO CREATE THIS ACCESSORY YOU WILL NEED

25g Fudge, 25g Silver

1 x 15cm (6in) Dowel

Handle

Working in Fudge

Begin by dc6 into ring

Rnds 1-22 dc (22 rnds)

Break yarn. Insert dowel and gather stitches to close.

Blade

Working in Silver

Begin by dc4 into ring

Rnds 1-3 dc (3 rnds)

Rnd 4 dc2 into next st, dc3 (5)

Rnd 5 dc2 into next st, dc4 (6)

Rnd 6 dc2 into next st, dc5 (7)

Rnd 7 dc2 into next st, dc6 (8)

Rnd 8 dc2 into next st, dc7 (9)

Rnd 9 dc2 into next st, dc8 (10)

Rnd 10 dc3, ch2, miss 2, dc3, ch2, miss 2 (10)

Rnd 11 dc

Rnds 12-17 dc2tog, dc to end of rnd (6 rnds) (4 sts)

Rnds 18-19 dc (2 rnds)

Break yarn.

Stuff the blade through the chain hole and push the handle through the hole to join.

Dwarves from right to left: Malar, Gim, Tal, Hellir, Chlud, Stein, Brot.

Seven Dwarves

Instructions for individual dwarves will refer back to these shared patterns. Dwarves are named in the order that they appear in image on previous page.

Feet (make two)

Begin by dc6 into ring

Rnd 1 (dc1, dc2 into next st) 3 times (9)

Rnd 2 (dc2, dc2 into next st) 3 times (12)

Rnd 3 (dc3, dc2 into next st) 3 times (15)

Rnd 4 dc

Rnd 5 (dc4, dc2 into next st) 3 times (18)

Rnds 6-7 dc (2 rnds)

Rnd 8 ch5, miss 5, dc13 (18)

Rnd 9 dc

Rnd 10 (dc2tog) 9 times (9)

Rnd 11 (dc1, dc2tog) 3 times (6)

Break yarn.

Legs (make two)

Rejoin and work 10 sts around the hole in foot (work along the front of the opening first)

Rnds 1-2 dc (2 rnds)

Rnd 3 (dc2 into next st, dc4) twice (12)

Rnds 4-6 dc (3 rnds)

Rnd 7 (dc2 into next st, dc3) 3 times (15)

Rnds 8-9 dc (2 rnds)

Rnd 10 (dc2 into next st, dc4) 3 times (18)

Rnd 11 dc

Rnd 12 (dc2, dc2 into next st) 6 times (24)

Break yarn.

Body & Head

Lay legs side by side with feet facing downwards (legs are identical so there is no specific left or right).

Starting in the centre between the legs, insert hook into the side of first leg and work as follows:

Rnd 1 dc24 around first leg, dc24 around second leg (48)

Continue to work this 48-st round as follows:

Rnd 2 (dc2 into next st, dc7) 6 times (54)

Rnds 3-6 dc (4 rnds)

Rnd 7 dc3, (dc1, dc2tog) 3 times, dc30, (dc2tog, dc1) 3 times, dc3 (48)

Rnds 8, 10, 12 , 14 dc

Rnd 9 (dc2tog, dc6) 6 times (42)

Rnd 11 (dc2tog, dc5) 6 times (36)

Rnd 13 (dc2tog, dc4) 6 times (30)

Rnd 15 (dc2tog, dc3) 6 times (24)

Rnds 16-17 dc (2 rnds)

Rnd 18 (dc2tog) 12 times (12)

Rnds 19-20 dc (2 rnds)

Rnd 21 (dc2 into next st) 12 times (24)

Rnd 22 dc12, (dc2 into next st) 3 times, dc9 (27)

Rnd 23 (dc2, dc2 into next st) 9 times (36)

Rnd 24 (dc5, dc2 into next st) 6 times (42)

Rnds 25-27 dc (3 rnds)

Rnd 28 dc21, dc2tog, dc4, dc2tog, dc13 (40)

Rnds 29-30 dc (2 rnds)

Rnd 31 dc22, ch4, miss 4, dc14 (40)

Rnds 32-36 dc (5 rnds)

Rnd 37 (dc2, dc2tog) 10 times (30)

Rnd 38 dc

Rnd 39 (dc3, dc2tog) 6 times (24)

Rnd 40 (dc2, dc2tog) 6 times (18)

Rnd 41 (dc1, dc2tog) 6 times (12)

Rnd 42 (dc2, dc2tog) 3 times (9)

Stuff and gather remaining stitches to close.

Arms (make two)

Begin by dc6 into ring

Rnd 1 (dc2 into next st) 6 times (12)

Rnd 2 (dc3, dc2 into next st) 3 times (15)

Rnds 3-6 dc (4 rnds)

Rnd 7 dc6, (dc1, dc2tog) 3 times (12)

Rnds 8-9 dc (2 rnds)

Rnd 10 dc6, (dc1, dc2tog) twice (10)

Rnds 11-18 dc (8 rnds)

Rnd 19 (dc3, dc2tog) twice (8)

Rnd 20 dc

Stuff hand and sew flat across top to close.

Tunic

Ch25 and slst to join into a circle

Rnd 1 (dc2 into next st) 25 times (50)

Rnds 2-3 dc (2 rnds)

Rnd 4 miss 12 sts for armhole, dc13, miss 12 sts for other armhole, dc13 (26)

Continue to work central 26-st rnd as follows:

Rnd 1 dc2 into next st, dc11, (dc2 into next st) twice, dc11, dc2 into next st (30)

Rnd 2 dc

Rnd 3 (dc2 into next st, dc4) 6 times (36)

Rnd 4 dc

Rnd 5 (dc2 into next st, dc5) 6 times (42)

Rnd 6 dc

Rnd 7 (dc2 into next st, dc6) 6 times (48)

Rnd 8 dc

Rnd 9 (dc2 into next st, dc7) 6 times (54)

Rnds 10-14 dc (5 rnds)

Rnd 15 (dc7, dc2tog) 6 times (48)

Rnds 16-19 dc (4 rnds)

Break yarn.

Sleeves - rejoin and work both 12-st armholes as follows:

Rnds 1-8 dc (8 rnds)

Rnd 9 (dc3, dc2 into next st) 3 times (15)

Rnd 10 (dc4, dc2 into next st) 3 times (18)

Break yarn.

Jumper

Ch25 and sl st to join into a circle

Rnd 1 (dc2 into next st) 25 times (50)

Rnds 2-3 dc (2 rnds)

Rnd 4 miss 12 sts for armhole, dc13, miss 12 sts for other armhole, dc13 (26)

Continue to work central 26-st rnd as follows:

Rnd 1 dc2 into next st, dc11, (dc2 into next st) twice, dc11, dc2 into next st (30)

Rnds 2, 4, 6, 8 dc

Rnd 3 (dc2 into next st, dc4) 6 times (36)

Rnd 5 (dc2 into next st, dc5) 6 times (42)

Rnd 7 (dc2 into next st, dc6) 6 times (48)

Rnd 9 (dc2 into next st, dc7) 6 times (54)

Rnds 10-12 dc (3 rnds)

Rnd 13 tr

Rnd 14 (FPtr1, BPtr1) 27 times

Break yarn.

Sleeves - rejoin and work both 12-st armholes as follows:

Rnds 1-8 dc (8 rnds)

Rnd 9 (dc3, dc2 into next st) 3 times (15)

Rnd 10 tr14, tr2 into the next (16)

Rnd 11 (FPtr1, BPtr1) 8 times

Break yarn.

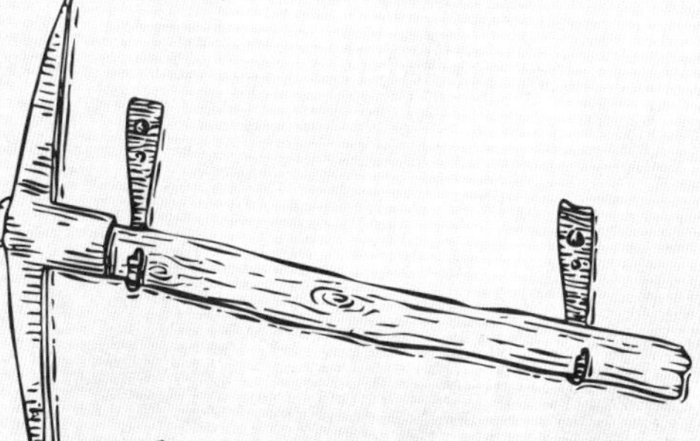

Shorts

Ch48 and sl st to join into a circle

Rnds 1-8 dc (8 rnds)

Split into two rounds of 24 sts and work each as follows:

Rnds 1-2 dc (2 rnds)

Break yarn.

Boots (make two)

Begin by dc6 into ring

Rnd 1 (dc2 into next st) 6 times (12)

Rnd 2 (dc3, dc2 into next st) 3 times (15)

Rnd 3 (dc4, dc2 into next st) 3 times (18)

Rnds 4-9 dc (6 rnds)

Rnd 10 ch5, miss 5, dc13 (18)

Rnd 11 dc

Rnd 12 (dc2tog) 9 times (9)

Rnd 13 (dc1, dc2tog) 3 times (6)

Break yarn.

Pointed Boots (make two)

Begin by dc6 into ring

Rnds 1-3 dc (3 rnds)

Rnd 4 (dc1, d2 into next st) 3 times (9)

Rnd 5 dc

Rnd 6 (dc2, dc2 into next st) 3 times (12)

Rnd 7 dc

Rnd 8 (dc3, dc2 into next st) 3 times (15)

Rnd 9 (dc4, dc2 into next st) 3 times (18)

Rnds 10-13 dc (4 rnds)

Rnd 14 ch5, miss 5, dc13 (18)

Rnd 15 dc

Rnd 16 (dc2tog) 9 times (9)

Rnd 17 (dc1, dc2tog) 3 times (6)

Break yarn.

Rejoin and work 10 sts around the hole in foot (work along the front of the opening first)

Rnd 1 dc

Rnd 2 (dc2 into next st, dc4) twice (12)

Rnd 3 (dc2 into next st, dc2) 4 times (16)

Break yarn.

Pointed Hat

Begin by dc6 into ring

Rnds 1-3 dc (3 rnds)

Rnd 4 dc2 into next st, dc5 (7)

Rnds 5-6 dc (2 rnds)

Rnd 7 dc2 into next st, dc6 (8)

Rnds 8-9 dc (2 rnds)

Rnd 10 dc2 into next st, dc7 (9)

Rnds 11, 13, 15, 17, 19, 21, 23, 25 dc

Rnd 12 (dc2, dc2 into next st) 3 times (12)

Rnd 14 (dc3, dc2 into next st) 3 times (15)

Rnd 16 (dc4, dc2 into next st) 3 times (18)

Rnd 18 (dc2, dc2 into next st) 6 times (24)

Rnd 20 (dc3, dc2 into next st) 6 times (30)

Rnd 22 (dc4, dc2 into next st) 6 times (36)

Rnd 24 (dc5, dc2 into next st) 6 times (42)

Rnd 26 (dc6, dc2 into next st) 6 times (48)

Rnds 27-33 dc (7 rnds)

Break yarn.

Bandana

Begin by dc6 into ring

Rnd 1 dc

Rnd 2 (dc2, dc2 into next st) twice (8)

Rnd 3 (dc3, dc2 into next st) twice (10)

Rnd 4 (dc4, dc2 into next st) twice (12)

Rnd 5 (dc2 into next st, dc4, dc2 into next st) twice (16)

Rnd 6 (dc2 into next st, dc6, dc2 into next st) twice (20)

Rnd 7 (dc2 into next st, dc8, dc2 into next st) twice (24)

Rnd 8 (dc2 into next st, dc10, dc2 into next st) twice (28)

Rnd 9 (dc2 into next st, dc12, dc2 into next st) twice (32)

Rnd 10 (dc2 into next st, dc14, dc2 into next st) twice (36)

Rnd 11 (dc2 into next st, dc16, dc2 into next st) twice (40)

Rnd 12 (dc2 into next st, dc18, dc2 into next st) twice (44)

Rnd 13 (dc2 into next st, dc20, dc2 into next st) twice (48)

Fold flat and dc24 through both sides to close.

Ch24 and sl st to corner at other side of triangle, then work dc around all edges of the bandana.

MALAR THE DWARF

TO CREATE THIS CHARACTER YOU WILL NEED

50g Skin Tone (Fudge), 25g Hair Colour (Shale), 25g Sage, 25g Chive, 25g Cocoa

Legs

Work **Feet** and Rnds 1-3 of **Legs** in Chive before changing to Skin Tone

Body & Head

Working in Skin Tone, work **Body & Head** with MAKE BOBBLE (MB) nose as follows:

Rnd 31 dc22, MB(3), MB(6), miss 1, MB(3), dc14

Rnd 32 dc23, dc2 into top of large bobble, dc15

Beard & Hair

Working in Hair Colour

Using KNOT LENGTHS add long 30cm (12in) lengths to beard and head with shorter 6cm (2½in) lengths for moustache *(see Hairstyles)*.

Shorts

Work **Shorts** in Cocoa

Jumper

Work **Jumper** in Sage

Working in Cocoa, embroider FERN MOTIFS around the bottom of the jumper above the rib.

Boots (make two)

Work **Boots** in Cocoa

Working in Chive, rejoin and work 10 sts around hole in foot (work along front of opening first)

Rnd 1 tr

Rnd 2 (FPtr1, BPtr1) 5 times

Break yarn.

Hat

Work **Pointed Hat** in Chive

GIM THE DWARF

TO CREATE THIS CHARACTER YOU WILL NEED

50g Skin Tone (Camel), 25g Hair Colour (Cream), 25g Kale, 25g Green, 25g Mushroom

Body & Head

Working in Skin Tone, changing to Mushroom after Rnd 4 and back to Skin Tone after Rnd 18.

Nose

Working in Skin Tone

Rejoin and work 8 sts around the hole in the centre of the head

Rnds 1-2 dc (2 rnds)

Rnd 3 (dc2 into next st) 8 times (16)

Rnd 4 (dc2, dc2tog) 4 times (12)

Rnd 5 (dc2tog) 6 times (6)

Gather remaining stitches to close.

Beard

Working in Hair Colour

Work moustache as a row of ch7 SLIP CHAINS

Beneath the moustache create a triangular shaped beard with ch13 SLIP CHAINS in central longest point with ch11, ch8 and ch7 either side *(see Hairstyles).*

Eyebrows

Work four ch4 SLIP CHAINS with right side facing upwards.

Tunic

Work **Tunic** in Kale, changing to Green after Rnd 14. Work sleeves in Kale.

Working in Kale, embroider BLANKET STITCH around the bottom edge of the tunic, 2 rnds deep and every 2 sts.

Plaited Belt

Working in Mushroom

Make three lengths of ch150. Knot together at one end and then plait together.

Place around the waist and tie to secure.

Pointed Boots (make two)

Work **Pointed Boots** in Mushroom

Working in Kale, embroider the FERN MOTIF onto the top of each boot.

Ribbed Hat

Working in Green

Ch48 and sl st to join into a circle

Rnd 1 htr

Rnds 2-4 (FPtr1, BPtr1) 24 times (3 rnds)

Rnd 5 (FPtr2tog, BPtr1, FPtr1, BPtr1) 8 times (32)

Rnds 6-9 (FPtr1, BPtr1) 16 times (4 rnds)

Rnd 10 (FPtr2tog, BPtr1, FPtr1, BPtr1, FPtr1, BPtr1) 4 times (24)

Rnd 11 (FPtr1, BPtr1) 12 times

Rnd 12 (FPtr2tog, BPtr1) 6 times (12)

Rnds 13-15 (FPtr1, BPtr1) 6 times (3 rnds)

Break yarn.

Edging - working in Kale, work a round of dc around the starting chain on hat.

Tal the Dwarf

TO CREATE THIS CHARACTER YOU WILL NEED

50g Skin Tone (Camel), 25g Hair Colour (Cocoa), 25g Kale, 25g Sapphire, 25g Cream

Body & Head

Working in Skin Tone, changing to Cream after Rnd 4 and back to Skin Tone after Rnd 18.

Arms

Working in Skin Tone, changing to Cream after Rnd 9

Cuffs - htr around the colour change line in Cream

Collar - sl st into centre front of neck and htr around the colour change line

Nose

Work as **Malar the Dwarf** in Skin Tone.

Hair

Working in Hair Colour use ch3 CHAIN LOOPS to cover the full head *(see Hairstyles).*

Beard

Working in Hair Colour use ch3 CHAIN LOOPS *(see Hairstyles).*

Shorts

Work **Shorts** in Sapphire

Working in Kale, embroider BLANKET STITCH around the bottom edge of the shorts, 2 rnds deep and every 2 sts.

Braces - working in Kale, sl st into back waistband of shorts at one side, ch21, sl st into front of shorts two rnds down from waistband and MAKE BOBBLE (3). Break yarn and repeat for other side.

Scarf

Working in Sapphire

Ch72 and miss 2, tr70 back down chain, then work a round of dc around all edges. Break yarn.

Bandana

Work **Bandana** in Kale, then work dc in Sapphire around all edges.

Working in Cream, embroider three FERN MOTIFS onto the bandana.

Boots (make two)

Work **Boots** in Kale

Leaving a 2-st gap at the front, rejoin and work 8 sts around the hole in foot as follows:

Row 1 (RS) (dc1, dc2 into next st) 4 times, turn (12)

Continue to work these 12 sts in rows using INVISIBLE ROWS on wrong side row if desired:

Row 2 (WS) (INV) dc12, turn

Row 3 (RS) dc12

Break yarn.

Laces - working in Sapphire, work two ch3 lines onto top of each boot.

Hellir the Dwarf

TO CREATE THIS CHARACTER YOU WILL NEED

50g Skin Tone (Oatmeal), 25g Hair Colour (Mushroom), 25g Sage, 25g Green, 25g Charcoal

Legs

Work **Feet** and Rnds 1-3 of **Legs** in Sage before changing to Skin Tone.

Body & Head

Working in Skin Tone, work **Body & Head** with nose as follows:

Rejoin and work 8 sts around the hole in the centre of the head

Rnd 1 dc2 into next st, dc2, (dc2 into next st) twice dc2, dc2 into next st (12)

Rnd 2 (dc1, dc2 into next st) 6 times (18)

Rnd 3 dc

Rnd 4 (dc2tog) 9 times (9)

Rnd 5 (dc1, dc2tog) 3 times (6)

Gather remaining stitches to close.

Beard

Working in Hair Colour

Work ch12 CHAIN LOOPS for moustache with ch25 in centre of beard *(see Hairstyles)*.

Work three rows of ch8 CHAIN LOOPS around back of head with two rows of ch12 CHAIN LOOPS beneath *(see Hairstyles)*.

Eyebrows

Work four ch6 CHAIN LOOPS above each eye.

Shorts

Work **Shorts** in Charcoal.

Jumper

Work **Jumper** in Green

Working in Sage, work a round of sl st around the bottom of the jumper and sleeves above the ribbing.

Boots (make two)

Work **Boots** in Charcoal

Working in Charcoal, rejoin and work 10 sts around the hole in foot (work along the front of the opening first)

Rnds 1-2 dc (2 rnds)

Change to Sage

Rnd 3 tr

Break yarn.

Working in Green, embroider FERN MOTIF onto the top of each boot.

Bandana

Work **Bandana** in Sage, then work a line of sl st in Charcoal around all edges.

Chlud the Dwarf

TO CREATE THIS CHARACTER YOU WILL NEED

50g Skin Tone (Chestnut), 25g Hair Colour (Charcoal), 25g Kale, 25g Chive, 25g Stone

Body & Head

Working in Skin Tone, changing to Stone after Rnd 4 and back to Skin Tone after Rnd 18.

Nose

Working in Skin Tone

Rejoin and work 8 sts around the hole in the centre of the head

Rnds 1-2 dc (2 rnds)

Rnd 3 (dc2 into next st) 8 times (16)

Rnd 4 (dc2, dc2tog) 4 times (12)

Rnd 5 (dc2tog) 6 times (6)

Gather remaining stitches to close.

Hair

Working in Hair Colour

Work ch4 SLIP CHAINS to cover the full head *(see Hairstyles).*

Beard

Working in Hair Colour

Work moustache as a row of ch5 SLIP CHAINS with two ch12 SLIP CHAINS rows beneath *(see Hairstyles).*

Tunic

Work **Tunic** in Kale, changing to Chive after Rnd 14. Work sleeves in Kale.

Working in Kale, embroider BLANKET STITCH around the bottom edge of the tunic, 2 rnds deep and every 2 sts.

Working in Chive, embroider FERN MOTIF onto each shoulder.

Knotted Belt

Working in Stone

Ch72 and sl st 71 back down chain

Knot around the waist and sew to secure.

Pointed Boots (make two)

Work **Pointed Boots** in Stone

Working in Kale, embroider BLANKET STITCH around the top edge of the boots, 2 rnds deep and every 2 sts.

Hat

Work **Ribbed Hat** as **Gim the Dwarf** in Chive

Edging - working in Stone, rejoin and work around the starting chain as follows:

Rnd 1 tr48

Rnd 2 (FPtr1, BPtr1) 24 times

Break yarn.

Stein the Dwarf

TO CREATE THIS CHARACTER YOU WILL NEED

50g Skin Tone (Oatmeal), 25g Hair Colour (Fudge), 25g Sapphire, 25g Chestnut, 25g Cream

Body & Head

Working in Skin Tone, changing to Cream after Rnd 4 and back to Skin Tone after Rnd 18.

Arms

Working in Skin Tone change to Cream after Rnd 9

Cuffs - htr around the colour change line in Cream

Nose

Work as **Gim the Dwarf** in Skin Tone.

Hair

Working in Hair Colour use CROCHETED CHAINS to create ringlets as follows:

Ch7 and (dc2 into next st) 6 times back down chain

Work three rows around the back of the hairline and five as the moustache *(see Hairstyles)*.

Beard

Working in Hair Colour work ringlets as follows in a line beneath the moustache

Ch13 and (dc2 into next st) 12 times back down chain

Shorts

Work **Shorts** in Chestnut.

Braces

Working in Chestnut

Ch72 and tr70 back down chain, then work a round of dc around all edges. Break yarn.

Working in Cream, work a line of sl st along both long edges.

Belt

Working in Sapphire

Ch50 and sl st to join into a circle

Rnd 1 htr

Break yarn and sew around waist.

Sew braces into position by folding them in half lengthways and sewing 10 central stitches to front waistband of shorts then cross over shoulders at the back and sew the ends 6 sts apart. Complete by adding belt loops in Cream with ch3 adding two at the front and then four at the back as a continuation of the slip stitch edge lines from the braces.

Boots (make two)

Work **Boots** in Sapphire

Working in Cream, rejoin and work 10 sts around the hole in foot (work along the front of the opening first)

Rnd 1 tr

Rnd 2 (FPtr1, BPtr1) 5 times

Break yarn.

Laces - working in Chestnut, work ch5 laces to create a cross onto the front of each shoe, sl st into boot between each ch5.

Hat

Work **Pointed Hat** in Sapphire

Working in Cream, embroider BLANKET STITCH around the bottom edge of the hat, 2 rnds deep and every 2 sts.

Brot the Dwarf

TO CREATE THIS CHARACTER YOU WILL NEED

50g Skin Tone (Oatmeal), 25g Hair Colour (Steel), 25g Kale, 25g Chive, 25g Fudge

Body & Head

Working in Skin Tone, changing to Fudge after Rnd 4 and back to Skin Tone after Rnd 18.

Nose

Working as **Hellir the Dwarf** in Skin Tone.

Beard

Working in Hair Colour use ch6 CHAIN LOOPS for moustache with two ch12 rows beneath for the beard *(see Hairstyles).*

Hair

Working in Hair Colour

Work three rows of ch12 CHAIN LOOPS around back of head *(see Hairstyles).*

Eyebrows

Working in Hair Colour

Work three ch8 CHAIN LOOPS above each eye *(see Hairstyles).*

Tunic

Work **Tunic** in Chive, changing to Kale after Rnd 14. Work sleeves in Chive.

Working in Chive, embroider BLANKET STITCH around the bottom edge of the tunic, 2 rnds deep and every 2 sts.

Knotted Belt

Working in Fudge

Ch72 and sl st 71 back down chain

Knot around the waist and sew to secure.

Boots

Work **Boots** in Fudge

Rejoin and work 10 sts around the hole in foot (work along the front of the opening first)

Rnd 1 dc

Rnd 2 (dc2 into next st, dc4) twice (12)

Rnd 3 (dc2 into next st, dc3) 3 times (15)

Break yarn.

Hat

Work **Pointed Hat** in Kale

Working in Fudge, embroider BLANKET STITCH around the bottom edge of the hat, 2 rnds deep and every 2 sts.

Poisoned Apple

TO CREATE THIS ACCESSORY YOU WILL NEED

25g Ruby, 25g Chive, 25g Chestnut

Apple

Begin by dc3 Ruby, dc3 Chive into ring

Rnd 1 (dc2 into next st) 3 times Ruby, (dc2 into next st) 3 times Chive (12)

Rnd 2 dc6 Ruby, dc6 Chive

Rnd 3 (dc1, dc2 into next st) 3 times Ruby, (dc1, dc2 into next st) 3 times Chive (18)

Rnds 4-5 dc9 Ruby, dc9 Chive (2 rnds)

Rnd 6 (dc2, dc2 into next st) 3 times Ruby, (dc2, dc2 into next st) 3 times Chive (24)

Rnds 7-8 dc12 Ruby, dc12 Chive (2 rnds)

Rnd 9 (dc2, dc2tog) 3 times Ruby, (dc2, dc2tog) 3 times Chive (18)

Rnd 10 (dc2tog) 4 times, dc1 Ruby, (dc2tog) 4 times, dc1 Chive (10)

Continue in Chive

Rnd 11 (dc2tog) 5 times (5)

Stuff and gather remaining stitches to close.

Stalk - working in Chestnut, sl st into centre of apple, ch6 and sl st 5 back down chain.

Roses

TO CREATE THIS SCENERY YOU WILL NEED

25g Ruby, 25g Cream, 25g Green

Roses

Working in either Ruby or Cream

Ch6 and work back down chain as follows:

Miss 2, (tr3 into next st) 4 times

Allow the piece to curl, then sl st into edge to secure the shape.

Break yarn and sew in all ends.

Individual Rose Stem - working in Green, sl st into bottom of flower, ch7 and sl st 2 back down chain, ch3 and sl st 1, dc1, sl st 4 back down chain.

Vine (make two full sets in Ruby and two half sets in Cream)

Make 12 flowers for a full vine and 6 for a half vine

Vine - working in Green

(Ch13, sl st into back of rose then sl st 4 back down chain) 6 times, ch11, sl st 6 back down chain, (ch4, sl st into back of rose then sl st 4 back down chain, sl st 9 along main chain) 5 times, sl st to end of main chain.

CHAPTER FIVE

HANSEL & GRETEL

Once upon a time there was a boy called Hansel and his sister Gretel who lived with their mother and father in a cottage. Times were very hard and the woodcutter and his wife struggled to put bread on the table for their family of four to eat.

One evening after another week of worry and woe the woman said to her husband.

"We cannot all-four live any longer on what we have. For us to survive just one more day we must say goodbye to the children. We have no choice but to lead them into the forest tomorrow for they will never find their way back to us."

Although reluctant the woodcutter could provide no alternative as to how they could continue to live as they were and so exhausted, and with a very heavy heart, he agreed.

Tossing and turning with hunger Hansel and Gretel had overheard the chilling conversation, and had time to devise a plan. In the quietest hours of the night Hansel crept outside the cottage and in the bright light of the moon filled his pockets with as many shining white pebbles as he could find. Weighed down by his burden but content he had a solution he stole back into bed alongside his sister and assured her to sleep soundly for he could outwit their parents.

The next morning the children were each given a small loaf of bread and the family set off deep into the woods. Dragging his heels behind his parents' pace, Hansel gradually emptied his pockets along the path, careful to ensure his pebbles were not noticed by anyone. Just as he had dropped the final pebble his father stopped and began to build a fire.

"Stay here while we go and work, and we'll return before dark."

The children dutifully sat down by the lit fire and watched their parents walk away.

Hansel and Gretel fell asleep and when they awoke it was darker than any darkness they had seen before. But then, as the clouds moved across the inky sky, a brilliant path lit up before them leading home through the woods, shining like freshly minted coins in the silvery moonlight.

When they knocked on the broken wooden door to the cottage their father scooped them up with relief and joy.

"What clever children to find your way back!" their mother exclaimed with a tight smile.

For a while the family continued to share what little they had between them, with each day their stomachs aching more than the last, until one day the children once again overheard whispers. Despite their father's objection, the next day they were to be led even deeper into the woods in the hope that this time they couldn't possibly find their way home. As soon as he knew everyone else was asleep Hansel leapt up to fill his pockets with pebbles. But alas, the door was locked, and as he lay back down on his thin mattress his mind searched for an idea that would lead them back once more.

The next morning the children were led deep into the trees, this time the path they took followed so many twists and turns that Gretel's feet began to grow weary and her eyes heavy. As he walked Hansel crumbled the last measly piece of bread given to him inside his pocket, and hung back to carefully drop a trail of breadcrumbs as he went. Finally they reached a clearing and as last time, their father lit a fire before he and his wife waved a hasty goodbye leaving Hansel and Gretel behind. Hungry and exhausted the children drifted off to sleep by the fire, reassured by the path of crumbs that could once again lead them home. Later that evening they awoke to the noise of the wind in the branches to find the fire had gone out, so began their search for the way home. But just like them, the birds of the forest had also had little to eat that year, and so no sooner had their footsteps faded into the forest than the path of breadcrumbs had disappeared.

The children wandered through the trees for hours, hoping to stumble onto familiarity, when suddenly a white bird appeared on the path in front of them. Beckoning for them to follow it the bird took them even deeper into the woods. Just when the children felt like they could walk no further, there before them stood a cottage. This cottage was no ordinary cottage however, and as they walked closer they could smell that it was in fact made from sweet gingerbread and sugar. Overcome with hunger the children began to break off handfuls of the walls and devour the sweet and sticky bread as fast as they could, when the door opened and an old woman greeted them with a crooked smile.

"Come in, come in little ones, for there is plenty more to eat inside. You must be weary and I've got two perfect little beds for you to rest your heads."

Following their welcoming host inside the cottage, Hansel and Gretel were greeted with tables laden with treats, two plate settings neatly laid out for them, and in the corner two little crisp white beds bulging with blankets and pillows. Having eaten and drank their fill the children fell into the beds and drifted off into a very deep sleep.

Hansel was first to wake the next morning to find himself inside a cage. Shouting to his sister, she awoke and became instantly aware of the cold stare of the old woman sitting at a bare table that was the day before so burdened.

"You belong to me now," said the woman. "The boy will be fattened until he's good enough to eat, and you, girl, will help me do it."

Over the following weeks Hansel grew fatter and fatter as the woman, who was surely a witch, instructed enslaved Gretel to endlessly prepare food for him, while she herself grew thinner having to live off only crab shells. Each day the half-sighted witch would ask Hansel to stick his finger through the bars so she could feel when he would be ready to eat. For a whole month Hansel would carefully hold a bone up his sleeve and poke it out for inspection until one day, impatient and exasperated, the witch demanded Gretel prepare the oven, for she had been waiting long enough.

With the fire roaring the witch coaxed Gretel to open up the door and take a look inside to check that it was hot enough. Sensing the witch's intent Gretel pretended she didn't understand what had been asked, and coaxed the frustrated witch to show her. Seizing the moment as the witch leaned into the oven, Gretel shoved her head-first into it with all her might and slammed the heavy door behind her.

With the witch burning to death Gretel quickly released her brother from his cage, together they filled their pockets with the pearls and jewels Gretel had spotted filling every drawer, and they bolted through the open door. They ran as fast as they could away from the cottage in the woods, not really knowing which way they were heading but knowing that all paths away from the witch were better than what lay behind them.

Eventually they came to a river so wide that they could not swim across it, but they somehow both knew that home lay just beyond the far bank. Beckoning over to a white duck in amongst the reeds, the children asked for a ride over to the other side. Acquiescing their request, the children climbed one at a time between the duck's wings and were safely carried over the water. Having thanked the duck they clambered up onto the bank and quickly found the familiar path from the river bank that led straight to their front door. Back in their own cottage they found their father withered with grief and guilt and living alone, their mother having died in their absence. Together they all lived happily ever after with the wealth of the old witch, the children's shared ingenuity and the love of their father.

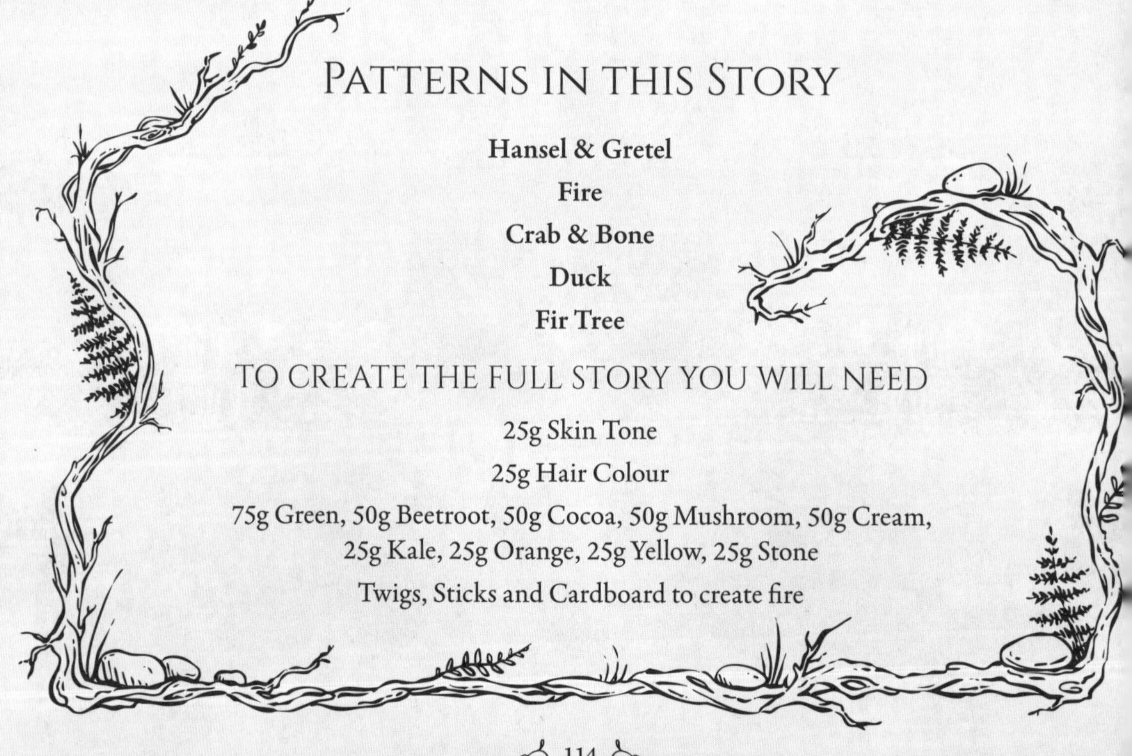

Patterns in this Story

Hansel & Gretel

Fire

Crab & Bone

Duck

Fir Tree

To Create the Full Story You Will Need

25g Skin Tone

25g Hair Colour

75g Green, 50g Beetroot, 50g Cocoa, 50g Mushroom, 50g Cream, 25g Kale, 25g Orange, 25g Yellow, 25g Stone

Twigs, Sticks and Cardboard to create fire

Hansel

TO CREATE THIS CHARACTER YOU WILL NEED

25g Skin Tone (Camel), 25g Hair Colour (Stone), 25g Beetroot, 25g Kale, 25g Mushroom, 25g Cocoa, 25g Cream

Body & Head

Working in Cocoa

Ch6 and work around chain as follows:

Rnd 1 dc4, dc2 into next st along one side of chain, dc4, dc2 into next st along other side of chain (12)

Rnd 2 (dc2 into next st) 12 times (24)

Rnds 3-8 dc (6 rnds)

Change to Beetroot

Rnd 9 (dc4, dc2tog) 4 times (20)

Rnd 10 dc

Rnd 11 (dc4, dc2 into next st) 4 times (24)

Rnds 12-15 dc (4 rnds)

Rnd 16 (dc2tog) 4 times, dc3, (dc2tog) 4 times, dc3, dc2tog (15)

Change to Skin Tone

Rnd 17 (dc2tog) 7 times, dc1 (8)

Rnd 18 dc

Rnd 19 dc2, dc3 into next st, dc5 (10)

Rnd 20 dc2 into next st, dc2, (dc2 into next st) 3 times, dc2, dc2 into next st, dc1 (15)

Rnd 21 (dc2 into next st) 15 times (30)

Rnds 22-23 dc (2 rnds)

Rnd 24 dc10, (dc2tog) 4 times, dc12 (26)

Rnds 25-30 dc (6 rnds)

Rnd 31 (dc2tog) 13 times (13)

Rnd 32 (dc2tog) 6 times, dc1 (7)

Stuff and gather remaining stitches to close.

Arms (make two)

Working in Kale

Begin by dc6 into ring

Rnd 1 (dc1, dc2 into next st) 3 times (9)

Rnds 2-5 dc (4 rnds)

Rnd 6 (dc1, dc2tog) 3 times (6)

Change to Beetroot

Rnds 7-11 dc (5 rnds)

Rnd 12 dc2 into next st, dc5 (7)

Rnds 13-14 dc (2 rnds)

Rnd 15 dc2 into next, dc6 (8)

Rnds 16-20 dc (5 rnds)

Stuff hand and sew flat across top to close.

Legs (make two)

Working in Cream

Ch9 and work around chain as follows:

Rnd 1 dc7, dc2 into next st along one side of chain, dc7, dc2 into next st along other side of chain (18)

Rnds 2-3 dc (2 rnds)

Rnd 4 (dc2tog) 3 times, dc6, (dc2tog) 3 times (12)

Rnd 5 (dc2tog) twice, dc4, (dc2tog) twice (8)

Rnds 6-7 dc (2 rnds)

Rnd 8 dc4 Cream, dc4 Skin Tone

Continue in Skin Tone

Rnd 9 dc2 into next st, dc7 (9)

Rnds 10-11 dc (2 rnds)

Change to Cocoa

Rnd 12 dc

Rnd 13 dc2 into next st, dc8 (10)

Rnds 14-15 dc (2 rnds)

Stuff foot and sew flat across top to close.

Sew up your doll *(see Stuffing & Sewing Up)*.

Sew eyes into place with Black yarn and nose with Skin Tone yarn.

Working in Hair Colour use CHAIN LOOPS, working ch8 on the top of the head and ch6 around the back *(see Hairstyles)*.

Mittens - working in Kale, work a round of sl st around the colour change line on each arm.

Thumbs - working in Kale, sl st into thumb position, ch3 and sl st 2 back down chain, break yarn.

Socks - working in Cream, work a round of sl st around the colour change line between Cream and Skin Tone on each leg.

Shorts - working in Cocoa, work a round of sl st around the colour change line between Skin Tone and Cocoa on each leg.

Waistband - working in Cocoa, work a round of sl st around the top of waistband colour change line on body.

Belt - working in Mushroom, work a line of sl st around the top of the shorts on body, below the round of Cocoa worked previously.

Neckerchief

Working in Mushroom

Ch29 and sl st 28 back down chain

Place around the neck and tie at the front.

Shirt Collar - working in Beetroot, sl st into centre back of neck and work around colour change line towards the front as follows:

*dc3, htr2, tr2 into same st, sl st into body below over the neckerchief, break yarn.

Sl st into centre back of neck and repeat from * to work the other side.

Braces - working in Cocoa, sl st into front waistband of shorts at one side, ch16 and sl st into centre back of waistband, ch16 and sl st into front at other side. Break yarn.

Shoes (make two)

Working in Mushroom

Ch9 and work around chain as follows:

Rnd 1 dc7, dc2 into next st along one side of chain, dc7, dc2 into next st along other side of chain (18)

Rnd 2 dc2 into next st, dc15, dc2 into next st, dc1 (20)

Rnds 3-5 dc (3 rnds)

Rnd 6 (dc2tog) 3 times, dc8, (dc2tog) 3 times (14)

Break yarn.

Shoe Laces - working in Cocoa, sl st into front side of shoe, ch5 and sl st to other side, break yarn.

Hat

Working in Kale

Begin by dc6 into ring

Rnd 1 (dc2 into next st) 6 times (12)

Rnd 2 (dc1, dc2 into next st) 6 times (18)

Rnd 3 dc

Rnd 4 (dc2, dc2 into next st) 6 times (24)

Rnd 5 dc

Rnd 6 (dc3, dc2 into next st) 6 times (30)

Rnd 7 (dc4, dc2 into next st) 6 times (36)

Rnd 8 dc

Rnd 9 htr

Change to Beetroot

Rnds 10-11 (FPhtr1, BPhtr1) 18 times (2 rnds)

Break yarn.

Pom Pom - working in Beetroot, wrap multiple wraps of yarn around two fingers and secure by tying a knot around the middle, leaving a long end for sewing. Fluff-up and trim as desired and then sew into position on top of hat.

Jacket

Working in Cocoa

Ch27 and work in rows as follows using INVISIBLE ROWS technique on wrong side rows if desired:

Rows 1-13 dc26, turn (13 rows)

Continue working dc back and forth in rows as follows:

Work first 6 sts for 7 rows, break yarn.

Rejoin at next st and work central 14 sts for 7 rows, break yarn.

Rejoin at next st and work last 6 sts for 7 rows, break yarn.

Edging - working in Kale, work a row of sl st along the bottom starting chain edge of jacket, then continue to dc around all remaining edges.

Construction - fold the two outer rectangles inwards towards the centre and join the shoulder seams by sewing along the top on both sides.

Pockets (make two)

Working in Cocoa

Ch7 and work in rows as follows using INVISIBLE ROWS technique on wrong side rows if desired:

Rows 1-5 dc (5 rows)

Change to Kale

Row 6 dc

Sew into position on front of jacket.

Pebbles - working in Cream, embroider FRENCH KNOTS inside the pockets.

Fire

TO CREATE THIS SCENERY YOU WILL NEED

25g Yellow, 25g Orange

Sticks, Cardboard

Flames (make approx. five)

Working in Orange

Ch7 and sl st 3, dc1, htr2 back down chain

Change to Yellow and continue working along other side of chain as follows:

(htr2 into next st) twice, dc2, sl st 2

Ch4, sl st 3 back down chain and then continue to work around the edge as follows:

sl st 1, dc2, htr2, htr2 into next st

Break yarn.

Gather sticks and cut to various lengths between 2-6cm (1-2in). Cut a circle from cardboard approximately 5cm (2in) across and then glue the sticks onto the circle base to create your fire wood shape. Glue the crochet flames into position.

As an alternative to using sticks crochet five 'logs' using the **Axe Handle** pattern from Jack & the Beanstalk *(see Axe & Rucksack)*.

Gretel

TO CREATE THIS CHARACTER YOU WILL NEED

25g Skin Tone (Camel), 25g Hair Colour (Stone), 25g Beetroot, 25g Kale, 25g Mushroom, 25g Cocoa, 25g Cream

Body & Head

Working in Cocoa

Ch6 and work around chain as follows:

Rnd 1 dc4, dc2 into next st along one side of chain, dc4, dc2 into next st along other side of chain (12)

Rnd 2 (dc2 into next st) 12 times (24)

Rnds 3-8 dc (6 rnds)

Change to Cream

Rnd 9 (dc4, dc2tog) 4 times (20)

Rnd 10 dc

Rnd 11 (dc4, dc2 into next st) 4 times (24)

Rnds 12-15 dc (4 rnds)

Rnd 16 (dc2tog) 4 times, dc3, (dc2tog) 4 times, dc3, dc2tog (15)

Rnd 17 (dc2tog) 7 times, dc1 (8)

Change to Skin Tone

Rnd 18 dc

Rnd 19 dc2, dc3 into next st, dc5 (10)

Rnd 20 dc2 into next st, dc2, (dc2 into next st) 3 times, dc2, dc2 into next st, dc1 (15)

Rnd 21 (dc2 into next st) 15 times (30)

Rnds 22-23 dc (2 rnds)

Rnd 24 dc10, (dc2tog) 4 times, dc12 (26)

Rnds 25-30 dc (6 rnds)

Rnd 31 (dc2tog) 13 times (13)

Rnd 32 (dc2tog) 6 times, dc1 (7)

Stuff and gather remaining stitches to close.

Arms (make two)

Working in Skin Tone

Begin by dc6 into ring

Rnd 1 (dc1, dc2 into next st) 3 times (9)

Rnds 2-5 dc (4 rnds)

Rnd 6 (dc1, dc2tog) 3 times (6)

Rnds 7-11 dc (5 rnds)

Rnd 12 dc2 into next st, dc5 (7)

Rnds 13-14 dc (2 rnds)

Change to Cream

Rnd 15 dc2 into next st, dc6 (8)

Rnds 16-17 dc (2 rnds)

Rnd 18 dc4, (dc2 into next st) 4 times (12)

Rnd 19 dc4, (dc1, dc2 into next st) 4 times (16)

Rnd 20 dc4, (dc3tog) 4 times (8)

Stuff hand and sew flat across top to close.

Legs (make two)

Working in Skin Tone

Ch9 and work around chain as follows:

Rnd 1 dc7, dc2 into next st along one side of chain, dc7, dc2 into next st along other side of chain (18)

Rnds 2-3 dc (2 rnds)

Rnd 4 (dc2tog) 3 times, dc6, (dc2tog) 3 times (12)

Rnd 5 (dc2tog) twice, dc4, (dc2tog) twice (8)

Rnds 6-8 dc (3 rnds)

Rnd 9 dc2 into next st, dc7 (9)

Rnds 10-12 dc (3 rnds)

Rnd 13 dc2 into next st, dc8 (10)

Rnds 14-15 dc (2 rnds)

Stuff foot and sew flat across top to close.

Sew up your doll *(see Stuffing & Sewing Up)*.

Sew eyes into place with Black yarn and nose with Skin Tone yarn.

Pigtails - working in Hair Colour use CHAIN LOOPS, work down the parting on either side to the pigtail point and then work three 20st chains to be plaited and tied to secure *(see Hairstyles)*.

Sleeve Frills - working in Cream, work a round of stitches around the colour change line on each arm as follows:

(ch3, sl st 1) 8 times, break yarn.

Collar - working in Cream, work a round of stitches around the colour change line on neck as follows:

sl st into centre front of neckline, ch3, tr1, htr1, dc3 around the back of the neck, htr1, tr1, ch2, sl st into centre front of neck. Break yarn.

Skirt

Working in Beetroot

Ch20 and sl st to join into a circle

Rnd 1 dc

Rnd 2 (dc2 into next st, dc4) 4 times (24)

Rnd 3 dc

Rnd 4 (dc2 into next st) 24 times (48)

Rnds 5-11 dc (7 rnds)

Change to Kale

Rnd 12 dc

Rnd 13 (ch3, miss 1, sl st 1) 24 times

Break yarn.

Pinafore Dress Top

Working in Kale

With the round end at the back and the right side facing, join yarn and dc9 along the front waistline of skirt

Turn and work these 9 sts in rows as follows using INVISIBLE ROWS technique on wrong side rows if desired:

Row 1 (WS) (INV) dc9, turn

Row 2 (RS) dc9, turn

Row 3 (WS) (INV) dc9, turn

Row 4 (RS) dc9, turn

Row 5 (WS) (INV) dc9

Do not break yarn.

Straps - working in Kale, place skirt with top onto doll, ch12, take over shoulder and sl st to waistline of skirt on opposite side, sl st 5 along back waistline of skirt, then ch12 and sl st to other side on the front of top. Break yarn.

Working in Stone, work a round of sl st around the colour change line at the bottom of the skirt.

Lacing - working in Stone, work ch3 laces in a cross formation onto the top section of the dress, sl st into the fabric between each ch3.

Apron

Working in Mushroom

Ch35 and work in rows as follows:

Row 1 dc22, turn

Row 2 dc10

Row 3 ch10, then create a 20-st rnd by dc10 along the main stitches

Place stitch marker and continue to work these 20 stitches in the round as follows:

Rnd 1 (dc2 into next st, dc9) twice (22)

Rnd 2 (dc2 into next st, dc10) twice (24)

Rnd 3 (dc2 into next st, dc11) twice (26)

Rnd 4 (dc2 into next st, dc12) twice (28)

Rnd 5 (dc2 into next st, dc13) twice (30)

Rnd 6 dc4 (incomplete rnd)

Fold flat and dc across the bottom through both sides to close. Break yarn.

Working in Mushroom, rejoin and dc12 along the remaining starting chain at the top.

Working in Kale, work a row of dc along the bottom edge.

Working in Cocoa, work a line of sl st across the top of the apron 'pocket', one row below the edge.

Place the apron onto the doll, tie around the waist and sew to secure.

Cloak

Working in Kale

Begin by dc6 into ring

Rnd 1 (dc2 into next st) 6 times (12)

Rnd 2 (dc1, dc2 into next st) 6 times (18)

Rnd 3 (dc2, dc2 into next st) 6 times (24)

Rnd 4 (dc3, dc2 into next st) 6 times (30)

Rnd 5 dc

Rnd 6 (dc4, dc2 into next st) 6 times (36)

Rnd 7 dc

Rnd 8 (dc5, dc2 into next st) 6 times (42)

Rnd 9 dc

Rnd 10 (dc6, dc2 into next st) 6 times (48)

Change to Beetroot and work in rows as follows using INVISIBLE ROWS technique on wrong side rows if desired:

Row 1 (RS) dc36, turn (36)

Row 2 (WS) (INV) dc36

Break yarn.

Working in Kale

Rejoin and work the remaining 12 sts in rows as follows using INVISIBLE ROWS technique on wrong side rows if desired:

Row 1 (RS) (dc2 into next st) 12 times (24)

Row 2 (WS) (INV) dc24

Row 3 (RS) (dc3, dc2 into next st) 6 times (30)

Row 4 (WS) (INV) dc30

Row 5 (RS) (dc4, dc2 into next st) 6 times (36)

Row 6 (WS) (INV) dc36

Row 7 (RS) (dc5, dc2 into next st) 6 times (42)

Row 8 (WS) (INV) dc42

Break yarn.

Ties - working in Kale, work a tie on either side of the cloak neckline as follows:

sl st into position, ch16 and sl st 15 back down chain, break yarn.

Edging - working in Beetroot, work two rounds of dc around the edges of the cloak.

Boots (make two)

Working in Cocoa

Ch9 and work around chain as follows:

Rnd 1 dc7, dc2 into next st along one side of chain, dc7, dc2 into next st along other side of chain (18)

Rnd 2 dc2 into next st, dc15, dc2 into next st, dc1 (20)

Rnds 3-5 dc (3 rnds)

Rnd 6 (dc2tog) 3 times, dc8, (dc2tog) 3 times (14)

Rnd 7 dc2tog, dc10, dc2tog (12)

Continue to work rows as follows:

Row 1 (RS) dc11, turn

Row 2 (WS) dc10, turn

Row 3 (RS) dc10

Break yarn.

Laces - working in Stone, work ch3 laces in a cross formation onto the front of each boot, sl st into boot between each ch3.

"Come in, come in little ones, for there is plenty more to eat inside. You must be weary and I've got two perfect little beds for you to rest your heads."

CRAB

TO CREATE THIS ACCESSORY YOU WILL NEED

25g Orange

Crab Underside

Working in Orange

Begin by dc6 into ring

Rnd 1 (dc2 into next st) 6 times (12)

Rnd 2 (dc1, dc2 into next st) 6 times (18)

Break yarn.

Crab Top Shell

Working in Orange

Begin by dc6 into ring

Rnd 1 (dc2 into next st) 6 times (12)

Rnd 2 (dc1, dc2 into next st) 6 times (18)

Rnd 3 dc

Continue to join the top shell to the underside with a round of dc from the bottom up, stuffing before fully closed.

Legs - working from the bottom up, sl st into edge of shell, ch4 and sl st 3 back down chain, sl st 1 along edge, ch4, and sl st 3 back down chain, sl st 1 along edge. Break yarn and repeat on other side.

Claws - working from the top down, sl st into edge of shell, ch9 and sl st 1, dc1, htr1 back down chain, ch4 and sl st 1, dc1, htr1, dc5 back down chain to bottom. Break yarn and repeat for second claw.

BONE

TO CREATE THIS ACCESSORY YOU WILL NEED

25g Cream

Bone

Working in Cream

Ch7 and work back down chain as follows:

Miss 1, (MAKE BOBBLE(3), sl st 1, MAKE BOBBLE(3)) into next st, sl st 4 along chain, (MAKE BOBBLE(3), sl st 1, MAKE BOBBLE(3)) into next st

Break yarn.

Duck

TO CREATE THIS CHARACTER YOU WILL NEED

50g Cream, 25g Stone, 25g Orange, 25g Cocoa

3 x Centralisers

Body, Neck & Head

Working in Stone

Begin by dc6 into ring

Rnd 1 (dc2 into next st) 6 times (12)

Rnd 2 (dc1, dc2 into next st) 6 times (18)

Rnd 3 (dc2, dc2 into next st) 6 times (24)

Rnd 4 (dc3, dc2 into next st) 6 times (30)

Rnd 5 (dc4, dc2 into next st) 6 times (36)

Rnd 6 (dc5, dc2 into next st) 6 times (42)

Change to Cream

Rnd 7 (dc1 SPIKE STITCH two rnds below, dc3, dc1 SPIKE STITCH two rnds below, dc1, dc2 into next st) 6 times (48)

Rnd 8 (dc7, dc2 into next st) 6 times (54)

Rnd 9 (dc8, dc2 into next st) 6 times (60)

Change to Stone

Rnd 10 (dc2, dc1 SPIKE STITCH three rnds below) 20 times

Rnds 11-12 dc (2 rnds)

Change to Cream

Rnd 13 (dc1 SPIKE STITCH three rnds below, dc3) 15 times

Rnds 14-16 dc (3 rnds)

Rnd 17 dc6, place centraliser, dc21, (dc2 into next st) 6 times, dc22, place centraliser, dc5 (66)

Rnd 18 dc21, (dc2tog) 3 times, dc12, (dc2tog) 3 times, dc21 (60)

Rnd 19 dc18, place centraliser, dc24 (incomplete rnd)

Split the 24 stitches marked with your centraliser into the round and work this 24-st round as follows.

Rnds 20-21 dc (2 rnds)

Rnd 22 dc2tog, dc20, dc2tog (22)

Rnd 23 dc

Rnd 24 dc2tog, dc18, dc2tog (20)

Rnd 25 dc8, (dc2tog) twice, dc8 (18)

Rnd 26 dc8, (dc2tog) twice, dc6 (16)

Rnds 27-28 dc (2 rnds)

Rnd 29 dc6, (dc2 into next st) 9 times, dc1 (25)

Rnd 30 dc11, (dc2 into next st) 5 times, dc9 (30)

Rnds 31-36 dc (6 rnds)

Rnd 37 (dc3, dc2tog) 6 times (24)

Rnd 38 dc

Rnd 39 (dc2, dc2tog) 6 times (18)

Rnd 40 (dc1, dc2tog) 6 times (12)

Rnd 41 (dc2, dc2tog) 3 times (9)

Gather remaining stitches to close.

Stuff the body, neck and head and then fold the back opening flat and sew across to close.

“Together they all lived happily ever after with the wealth of the old witch, the children’s shared ingenuity and the love of their father.”

Wing Pattern One (make one in Stone and one in Cream)

Ch16 and sl st 1, dc1, htr1, tr2, dtr10 back down chain

Ch13 and sl st 1, dc1, htr1, tr2, dtr7 back down chain

Ch10 and sl st 1, dc1, htr1, tr2, dtr4 back down chain

Break yarn.

Wing Pattern Two (make one in Stone and one in Cream)

Ch10 and sl st 1, dc1, htr1, tr2, dtr4 back down chain

Ch13 and sl st 1, dc1, htr1, tr2, dtr7 back down chain

Ch16 and sl st 1, dc1, htr1, tr2, dtr10 back down chain

Break yarn.

Wing Edging - lay a Stone and Cream wing piece together, pairing up so that the prong lengths match with both pieces being right sides facing outwards. Working in Cream and with the Cream side of the wing facing you, dc around the edge through both pieces to join together.

Sew wings into position on either side of the body along the colour change line. Position each wing between the centralisers with the Cream sides facing outwards and the shorter prongs towards the front.

Beak

Working in Cocoa

Begin by dc6 into ring

Rnd 1 (dc1, dc2 into next st) 3 times (9)

Change to Orange

Rnd 2 (dc2, dc2 into next st) 3 times (12)

Rnds 3-7 dc (5 rnds)

Rnd 8 (dc2, dc2tog) 3 times (9)

Rnd 9 (dc2, dc2 into next st) 3 times (12)

Change to Cream

Rnd 10 (dc2 into next st) 12 times (24)

Do not stuff. Sew into position on head.

Feet (make two)

Working in Orange

Begin by dc6 into ring

Rnd 1 (dc2 into next st) 6 times (12)

Rnd 2 (dc3, dc2 into next st) 3 times (15)

Rnd 3 ch4, miss 4, dc2, (dc2, dc2 into next st) 3 times (18)

Rnd 4 (dc8, dc2 into next st) twice (20)

Rnd 5 dc

Rnd 6 (dc9, dc2 into next st) twice (22)

Rnd 7 dc

Rnd 8 (dc10, dc2 into next st) twice (24)

Rnds 9-11 dc (3 rnds)

Split into three rnds of 8 sts and work each as follows:

Rnd 1 dc

Rnd 2 (dc2tog) 4 times (4)

Rnd 3 (dc2tog) twice (2)

Break yarn.

Legs (make two)

Working in Orange

Rejoin and work 8 sts around the hole in foot (work along the front of the opening first)

Rnds 1-5 dc (5 rnds)

Change to Stone

Rnd 6 (dc1, dc2 into next st) 4 times (12)

Rnds 7-10 dc (4 rnds)

Break yarn.

Lightly stuff feet and thighs and sew legs into position on bottom of body.

Finish by sewing eyes into place with Black yarn.

Fir Tree

TO CREATE THIS SCENERY YOU WILL NEED

75g Green

Tree

Working in Green

Begin by dc6 into ring

Rnd 1 dc

Rnd 2 (dc2 into next st, dc2) twice (8)

Continue working all odd rnds into the back loop only

Rnds 3 and all odd rnds dc

Rnd 4 (dc2 into next st, dc3) twice (10)

Rnd 6 (dc2 into next st, dc4) twice (12)

Rnd 8 (dc2 into next st, dc5) twice (14)

Rnd 10 (dc2 into next st, dc6) twice (16)

Rnd 12 (dc2 into next st, dc7) twice (18)

Rnd 14 (dc4, dc2 into next st, dc4) twice (20)

Rnd 16 (dc5, dc2 into next st, dc4) twice (22)

Rnd 18 (dc5, dc2 into next st, dc5) twice (24)

Rnd 20 (dc6, dc2 into next st, dc5) twice (26)

Rnd 22 (dc6, dc2 into next st, dc6) twice (28)

Rnd 24 (dc7, dc2 into next st, dc6) twice (30)

Rnd 26 (dc7, dc2 into next st, dc7) twice (32)

Rnd 28 (dc8, dc2 into next st, dc7) twice (34)

Rnd 30 (dc8, dc2 into next st, dc8) twice (36)

Rnd 32 (dc9, dc2 into next st, dc8) twice (38)

Rnd 34 (dc9, dc2 into next st, dc9) twice (40)

Continue working through full stitch

Rnd 35 dc

Rnd 36 (dc10, dc2 into next st, dc9) twice (42)

Rnd 37 dc

Break yarn.

Working from the top down, work along the spiral of front loop stitches working the following branch pattern repeated throughout.

Branch - ch4 and htr1, dc2 back down chain, sl st into original stitch at base of chain, sl st 2 along spiral.

Base

Begin by dc6 into ring

Rnd 1 (dc2 into next st) 6 times (12)

Rnd 2 (dc1, dc2 into next st) 6 times (18)

Rnd 3 (dc2, dc2 into next st) 6 times (24)

Rnd 4 (dc3, dc2 into next st) 6 times (30)

Rnd 5 (dc4, dc2 into next st) 6 times (36)

Rnd 6 (dc5, dc2 into next st) 6 times (42)

Continue to join the base to the tree with a round of dc from the bottom up, stuffing before fully closed.

NOTE: the tree can be varied in size to create a display or a forest by only working the first section of the pattern until you have the number of stitches in the end of a row of the base, e.g. 24, 30, 36. Equally larger trees can be made by continuing the pattern upwards to 48, 56, 60.

CHAPTER SIX

Elves & the Shoemaker

One crisp autumn night a long time ago a hard-working shoemaker took his last pieces of leather from a drawer and set about cutting out the familiar shapes to be ready to make one final pair of shoes the next morning. Times had grown hard and his hands ached and creaked, never managing to move as fast as they once did when he was a younger man. He and his wife had become so poor that he knew he needed to make and sell this pair of shoes so they would not have empty stomachs as they went to sleep tomorrow. He lay out the carefully cut pieces on his old bench, tidied his tools and blew out his candle before heading to bed.

Still groggy as he walked in early the next morning to return to his craft, he rubbed his eyes in disbelief as the pair of completed shoes sat on the table before him. He was astonished and knew not what to think about how the shoes came to be made. Picking them up in his hands, the stitching and finishing was the finest he had ever seen. Exquisite in detail and perfect in every way, the shoes were a masterpiece.

He had barely had a chance to finish admiring the handiwork himself, when the door swung open and a customer strode in at once spotting the brand new shoes upon the bench. Admiring their superb quality and design, the gentleman tipped out his purse, offering twice what was the customary price to secure ownership of the shoes.

With the money paid for the mysteriously-made shoes, the shoemaker could afford to buy leather for two more pairs. That night he set about delicately cutting the shapes just as he had done the night previously, and as he laid out the pieces ready for him to make the next day, he stopped for a moment before blowing out his candle to think about who might have made the shoes that had stood so faultlessly here on his workbench that morning.

When he awoke the next morning he was once again astounded to find both pairs of shoes had been made to the same astounding craftsmanship as the previous pair. The tiny stitches were beautifully even and straight, the minute nails had been hammered almost invisibly in place into the soles. Just as he turned them back over into place on the bench customers started to walk through his door, and as with the first pair these magnificent shoes fetched double what he would normally sell his shoes for.

That afternoon he bought leather for four more pairs of shoes, and late into the night he cut the shapes and meticulously laid them out on the bench. Again, the next morning he found all four pairs made by the time the sun had risen, and so it went on and on for weeks. Everything he cut out in the evening was magically made by the morning, customers queued at his door for a pair of the perfect new shoes and so soon he had managed to earn back both his reputation and wealth.

Not long before Christmas the shoemaker turned to his wife one night before blowing out his candle and said, "What do you think of us staying up tonight so we can see who it is who is lending us this helping hand?"

The woman liked the idea very much, and together they hid in the corner of the room invisible to view, eagerly watching the pieces of leather lying out on the bench in the moonlight.

As it struck midnight two scarcely-clad tiny men climbed up the table leg and set to work stitching, sewing and hammering with their tiny hands that could move so fast the shoemaker and his wife could not believe their eyes. They worked with such speed and dedication that they did not stop even for a blink of the eye until all the pairs were complete, then they downed their tools and ran out of sight off the table just as fast as they had appeared.

The next morning the woman said to her husband, "We owe much to these little men who helped us when we most needed it. They run about with rags on their backs while their hard work has led to us living in riches. Let us sew two tiny pairs of trousers and shirts, knit two little jumpers and make two pairs of shoes and hats for them to show our gratitude."

The man was very happy to make the gifts to thank the elves, and so the husband and wife set to their task.

Soon it was Christmas Eve, and when everything was ready they wrapped them up into tiny little presents and laid them out on the bench. Just as before, on the stroke of midnight the elves came out to get to work, but instead of cut leather they found the tiny little presents. Showing astonishment, glee and pride they opened them up to find beautiful little clothes and quickly put them on admiring their finery in the reflection of the window.

They jumped and skipped all over the table singing a song, and holding hands they danced out of the cottage into the night, never to be seen again.

Patterns in this Story

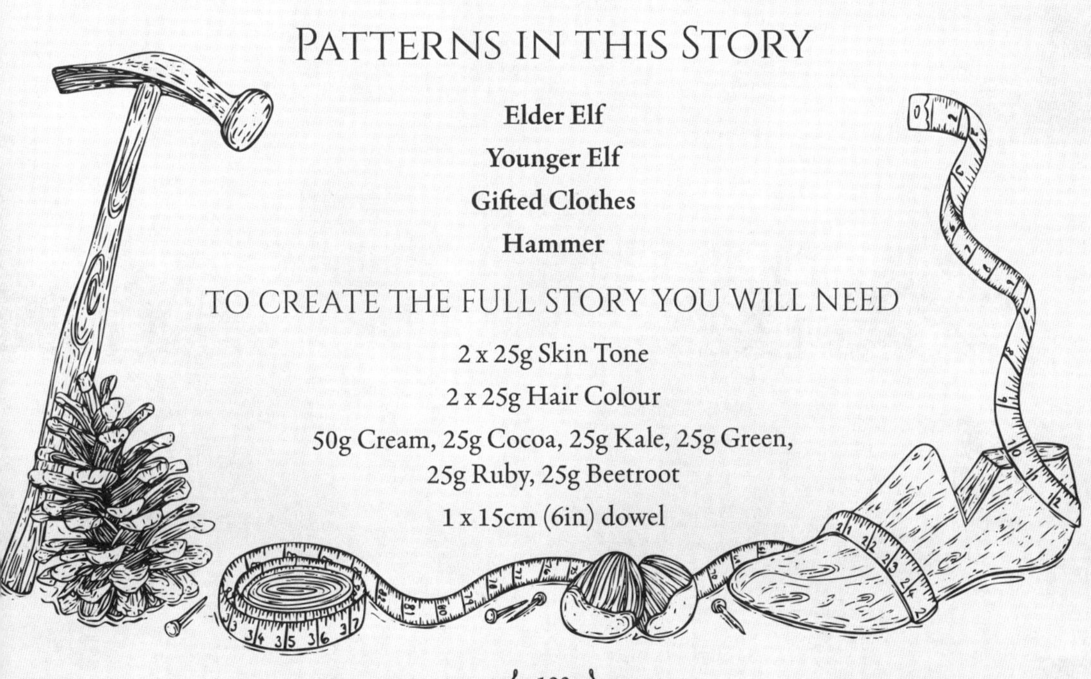

Elder Elf

Younger Elf

Gifted Clothes

Hammer

To Create the Full Story You Will Need

2 x 25g Skin Tone

2 x 25g Hair Colour

50g Cream, 25g Cocoa, 25g Kale, 25g Green, 25g Ruby, 25g Beetroot

1 x 15cm (6in) dowel

Elder Elf

TO CREATE THIS CHARACTER YOU WILL NEED

25g Skin Tone (Oatmeal), 25g Hair Colour (Silver), 25g Chestnut, 25g Cream, 25g Kale

Body & Head

Working in Kale

Ch6 and work around chain as follows:

Rnd 1 dc4, dc2 into next st along one side of chain, dc4, dc2 into next st along other side of chain (12)

Change to Cream

Rnd 2 (dc2 into next st) 12 times (24)

Rnd 3 dc

Change to Kale

Rnds 4-5 dc (2 rnds)

Change to Cream

Rnds 6-8 dc (3 rnds)

Rnd 9 (dc4, dc2tog) 4 times (20)

Rnd 10 dc

Rnd 11 (dc4, dc2 into next st) 4 times (24)

Rnds 12-15 dc (4 rnds)

Rnd 16 (dc2tog) 4 times, dc3, (dc2tog) 4 times, dc3, dc2tog (15)

Change to Skin Tone

Rnd 17 (dc2tog) 7 times, dc1 (8)

Rnd 18 dc

Rnd 19 dc2, dc3 into next st, dc5 (10)

Rnd 20 dc2 into next st, dc2, (dc2 into next st) 3 times, dc2, dc2 into next st, dc1 (15)

Rnd 21 (dc2 into next st) 15 times (30)

Rnds 22-23 dc (2 rnds)

Rnd 24 dc10, (dc2tog) 4 times, dc12 (26)

Rnds 25-30 dc (6 rnds)

Rnd 31 (dc2tog) 13 times (13)

Rnd 32 (dc2tog) 6 times, dc1 (7)

Stuff and gather remaining stitches to close.

Arms (make two)

Working in Skin Tone

Begin by dc6 into ring

Rnd 1 (dc1, dc2 into next st) 3 times (9)

Rnds 2-5 dc (4 rnds)

Rnd 6 (dc1, dc2tog) 3 times (6)

Rnds 7-11 dc (5 rnds)

Rnd 12 dc2 into next st, dc5 (7)

Rnds 13-14 dc (2 rnds)

Rnd 15 dc2 into next, dc6 (8)

Rnds 16-20 dc (5 rnds)

Stuff hand and sew flat across top to close.

Legs (make two)

Working in Cream

Ch9 and work around chain as follows:

Rnd 1 dc7, dc2 into next st along one side of chain, dc7, dc2 into next st along other side of chain (18)

Rnds 2-3 dc (2 rnds)

Rnd 4 dc4, (dc2tog) 3 times, dc7 Cream, dc1 Kale (15)

Continue in Kale

Rnd 5 dc2, (dc2tog) 5 times, dc3 (10)

Rnd 6 dc2, (dc2tog) twice, dc4 (8)

Change to Cream

Rnds 7-8 dc (2 rnds)

Continue working 2 rnds Kale, 2 rnds Cream

Rnd 9 dc7, dc2 into next st (9)

Rnds 10-12 dc (3 rnds)

Rnd 13 dc8, dc2 into next st (10)

Rnds 14 dc

Stuff foot and sew flat across top to close.

Ears (make two)

Working in Skin Tone

Begin by dc6 into ring

Rnd 1 (dc1, dc2 into next st) 3 times (9)

Rnds 2-3 dc (2 rnds)

Rnd 4 dc2tog, dc7 (8)

Rnd 5 dc2tog, dc6 (7)

Rnd 6 dc2tog, dc5 (6)

Rnd 7 dc2tog, dc4 (5)

Rnd 8 dc2tog, dc3 (4)

Do not stuff.

Sew up your doll *(see Stuffing & Sewing Up)*.

Sew eyes into place with Black yarn and nose with Skin Tone yarn.

Beard - working in Hair Colour use ch5 CHAIN LOOPS *(see Hairstyles)*.

Apron

Working in Kale

Ch24 and sl st to join into a circle

Rnds 1-13 dc (13 rnds)

Change to Chestnut

Rnd 14 htr

Break yarn.

Straps - working in Chestnut, sl st into top edge of apron, ch15 and sl st 14 back down chain, htr6 along top of apron, ch15 and sl st 14 back down chain, break yarn.

"The shoemaker lay out the carefully cut pieces on his old bench, tidied his tools and blew out his candle before heading to bed."

Hat

Working in Chestnut

Ch25 and work in rows using INVISIBLE ROWS technique on wrong side rows if desired:

Row 1 (RS) dc24, turn

Row 2 (WS) (INV) dc24, turn

Rows 3-10 repeat rows 1-2 four times (8 rows)

Row 11 (RS) dc24

Break yarn.

Fold one long edge of the panel in half and sew along the join to create the triangular shape.

Sl st into corner of hat, ch12 and work three ch3 CHAIN LOOPS into next st, sl st 10 back down chain, dc along edge of hat to other corner, ch12 and work three ch3 CHAIN LOOPS into next st, sl st 10 back down chain.

Sandals

Working in Chestnut

Ch9 and work around chain as follows:

Rnd 1 dc7, dc2 into next st along one side of chain, dc7, dc2 into next st along other side of chain (18)

Rnd 2 dc

Rnd 3 dc5, ch7 and sl st to opposite side of shoe

Break yarn. Sew into position on feet.

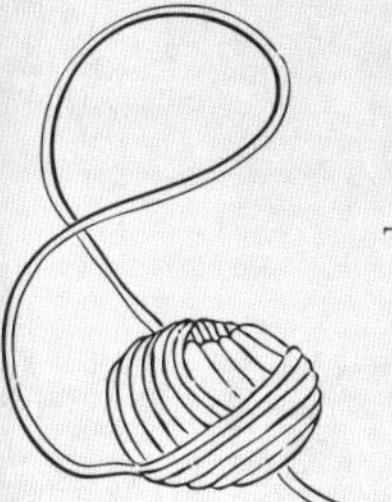

Younger Elf

TO CREATE THIS CHARACTER YOU WILL NEED

25g Skin Tone (Chestnut), 25g Hair Colour (Charcoal), 25g Shale, 25g Cream, 25g Green

Body & Head

Working in Green

Ch6 and work around chain as follows:

Rnd 1 dc4, dc2 into next st along one side of chain, dc4, dc2 into next st along other side of chain (12)

Rnd 2 (dc2 into next st) 12 times (24)

Rnd 3 dc

Rnds 4-5 dc (2 rnds)

Change to Cream

Rnds 6-7 dc (2 rnds)

Change to Green

Rnd 8 dc

Rnd 9 (dc4, dc2tog) 4 times (20)

Change to Cream

Rnd 10 dc

Rnd 11 (dc4, dc2 into next st) 4 times (24)

Change to Green

Rnds 12-13 dc (2 rnds)

Change to Cream

Rnds 14-15 dc (2 rnds)

Change to Green

Rnd 16 (dc2tog) 4 times, dc3, (dc2tog) 4 times, dc3, dc2tog (15)

Rnd 17 (dc2tog) 7 times, dc1 (8)

Change to Skin Tone

Rnd 18 dc

Rnd 19 dc2, dc3 into next st, dc5 (10)

Rnd 20 dc2 into next st, dc2, (dc2 into next st) 3 times, dc2, dc2 into next st, dc1 (15)

Rnd 21 (dc2 into next st) 15 times (30)

Rnds 22-23 dc (2 rnds)

Rnd 24 dc10, (dc2tog) 4 times, dc12 (26)

Rnds 25-30 dc (6 rnds)

Rnd 31 (dc2tog) 13 times (13)

Rnd 32 (dc2tog) 6 times, dc1 (7)

Stuff and gather remaining stitches to close.

Arms (make two)

Working in Skin Tone

Begin by dc6 into ring

Rnd 1 (dc1, dc2 into next st) 3 times (9)

Rnds 2-5 dc (4 rnds)

Rnd 6 (dc1, dc2tog) 3 times (6)

Change to Green

Rnds 7-8 dc (2 rnds)

Change to Cream

Rnds 9-10 dc (2 rnds)

Change to Green

Rnd 11 dc

Rnd 12 dc2 into next st, dc5 (7)

Change to Cream

Rnds 13-14 dc (2 rnds)

Change to Green

Rnd 15 dc2 into next, dc6 (8)

Rnd 16 dc

Change to Cream

Rnds 17-18 dc (2 rnds)

Change to Green

Rnds 19-20 dc (2 rnds)

Stuff hand and sew flat across top to close.

Legs (make two)

Working in Cream

Ch9 and work around chain as follows:

Rnd 1 dc7, dc2 into next st along one side of chain, dc7, dc2 into next st along other side of chain (18)

Rnds 2-3 dc (2 rnds)

Rnd 4 (dc2tog) 3 times, dc6, (dc2tog) 3 times (12)

Rnd 5 (dc2tog) twice, dc4, (dc2tog) twice (8)

Rnds 6-7 dc (2 rnds)

Rnd 8 dc4 Cream, dc4 Skin Tone

Continue in Skin Tone

Rnd 9 dc2 into next st, dc7 (9)

Rnds 10-11 dc (2 rnds)

Rnd 12 dc

Rnd 13 dc2 into next st, dc8 (10)

Rnds 14-15 dc (2 rnds)

Stuff foot and sew flat across top to close.

Ears (make two)

Working in Skin Tone

Begin by dc6 into ring

Rnd 1 (dc1, dc2 into next st) 3 times (9)

Rnds 2-3 dc (2 rnds)

Rnd 4 dc2tog, dc7 (8)

Rnd 5 dc2tog, dc6 (7)

Rnd 6 dc2tog, dc5 (6)

Rnd 7 dc2tog, dc4 (5)

Rnd 8 dc2tog, dc3 (4)

Do not stuff.

Sew up your doll *(see Stuffing & Sewing Up)*.

Sew eyes into place with Black yarn and nose with Skin Tone yarn.

Beard - working in Hair Colour use ch4 CHAIN LOOPS with three ch30 loops in central chain which are then plaited *(see Hairstyles)*.

Cuffs - working in Green, work a line of dc around the hand colour change line on each arm.

Shorts

Working in Shale

Ch24 and sl st to join into circle

Rnds 1-6 dc (6 rnds)

Split into two rnds of 12 sts and work each as follows:

Rnd 1 dc

Rnd 2 (dc1, htr1, dc1, sl st 1) 3 times

Break yarn.

Hat

Working in Shale

Begin by dc6 into ring

Rnds 1-3 dc (3 rnds)

Rnd 4 dc2 into next st, dc5 (7)

Rnds 5-15 dc2 into next st, dc to end of rnd (11 rnds) (18 sts)

Rnd 16 (dc5, dc2 into next st) 3 times (21)

Rnd 17 (dc6, dc2 into next st) 3 times (24)

Rnd 18 (dc7, dc2 into next st) 3 times (27)

Rnd 19 (dc8, dc2 into next st) 3 times (30)

Rnds 20-21 dc (2 rnds)

Change to Green

Rnd 22 sl st

Break yarn.

Bobble - working in Green, work five ch6 CHAIN LOOPS into top of hat.

Sandals

Working in Shale

Ch9 and work around chain as follows:

Rnd 1 dc7, dc2 into next st along one side of chain, dc7, dc2 into next st along other side of chain (18)

Rnd 2 dc

Rnd 3 dc5, ch7 and sl st to opposite side of shoe

Break yarn. Sew into position on feet.

Gifted Clothes

TO CREATE THESE ACCESSORIES YOU WILL NEED

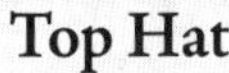

25g Ruby, 25g Beetroot, 25g Green, 25g Kale

Top Hat

Working in Beetroot

Begin by dc6 into ring

Rnd 1 (dc2 into next st) 6 times (12)

Rnd 2 (dc1, dc2 into next st) 6 times (18)

Rnd 3 (dc2, dc2 into next st) 6 times (24)

Rnd 4 (dc3, dc2 into next st) 6 times (30)

Rnd 5 tr

Rnds 6-13 dc (8 rnds)

Working into front loop only

Rnd 14 (dc2, dc2 into next st) 10 times (40)

Continue working through whole stitch

Rnd 15 (dc3, dc2 into next st) 10 times (50)

Rnd 16 dc

Break yarn.

Bowler Hat

Working in Ruby

Begin by dc6 into ring

Rnd 1 (dc2 into next st) 6 times (12)

Rnd 2 (dc1, dc2 into next st) 6 times (18)

Rnd 3 (dc2, dc2 into next st) 6 times (24)

Rnds 4-5 dc (2 rnds)

Rnd 6 (dc3, dc2 into next st) 6 times (30)

Rnds 7-8 dc (2 rnds)

Working into front loop only

Rnd 9 (dc2, dc2 into next st) 10 times (40)

Continue working through whole stitch

Rnd 10 dc

Break yarn.

Ribbon - working in Green, ch30 and sl st to join into a circle. Break yarn and sew into position on hat.

Jumper

Working in Beetroot

Ch18 and sl st to join into a circle

Rnd 1 dc

Rnd 2 (dc2 into next st) 18 times (36)

Rnd 3 (dc5, dc2 into next st) 6 times (42)

Rnd 4 miss 10 sts for armhole, dc11, miss 10 sts for other armhole, dc11 (22)

Continue to work central 22-st rnd as follows:

Rnd 1 (dc2 into next st, dc10) twice (24)

Rnds 2-13 dc (12 rnds)

Rnd 14 htr

Rnd 15 (FPhtr1, BPhtr1) 12 times

Break yarn.

Sleeves - rejoin and work both 10-st armholes as follows:

Rnds 1-12 dc (12 rnds)

Rnd 13 htr

Rnd 14 (FPhtr1, BPhtr1) 5 times

Break yarn.

Trousers

Working in Ruby

Ch24 and sl st to join into a circle

Rnds 1-6 dc (6 rnds)

Split into two rnds of 12 sts and rejoin and work each as follows:

Rnds 1-8 dc (8 rnds)

Break yarn.

Scarf

Working in Ruby

Ch38 and miss 2, tr36 back down chain

Break yarn and then add four knot lengths onto each end.

Boots (make two in Green and two in Kale)

Begin by dc6 into ring

Rnd 1 (dc1, dc2 into next st) 3 times (9)

Rnd 2 ch3, miss 3, dc6 (9)

Rnd 3 (dc1, dc2 into next st) 3 times, dc3 (12)

Rnd 4 (dc3, dc2 into next st) 3 times (15)

Rnds 5-7 dc (3 rnds)

Rnd 8 (dc3, dc2tog) 3 times (12)

Rnd 9 (dc2, dc2tog) 3 times (9)

Rnd 10 (dc1, dc2tog) 3 times (6)

Rnd 11 dc2tog, dc4 (5)

Rnd 12 dc2tog, dc3 (4)

Break yarn.

Rejoin and work 6 sts around the hole in foot (work along the front of the opening first)

Rnd 1 (dc1, dc2 into next st) 3 times (9)

Rnd 2 (dc2, dc2 into next st) 3 times (12)

Rnd 3 dc

Break yarn.

Finish with embroidery as desired (*see: Embroidery*).

Hammer

TO CREATE THIS ACCESSORY YOU WILL NEED

25g Mushroom, 25g Silver

1 x 15cm (6in) Dowel

Handle

Working in Mushroom

Begin by dc6 into ring

Rnds 1-12 dc (12 rnds)

Break yarn. Insert dowel (cut to 6cm (2½in)) and gather stitches to close.

Head Face

Working in Silver

Begin by dc6 into ring

Rnd 1 (dc1, dc2 into next st) 3 times (9)

Break yarn.

Head Neck

Working in Silver

Ch9 and sl st to join into a circle

Rnds 1-2 dc (2 rnds)

Rnd 3 dc2tog, dc7 (8)

Rnd 4 dc2tog, dc6 (7)

Rnd 5 dc2tog, dc5 (6)

Rnd 6 dc2tog, dc4 (5)

Rnd 7 dc2tog, dc3 (4)

Rnd 8 dc2tog, dc2 (3)

Do not break yarn. Stuff and continue to join the neck to the face with a round of dc.

Sew the head into position on the top of the handle.

TECHNICALS

In the following pages all the techniques and stitches used in this book are clarified from the very basics though to the most specific to these patterns. Someone completely new to crochet should first make the Golden Egg as a good introduction to 3D crochet *(see Reading a Pattern)*.

HOLDING YOUR HOOK AND YARN

There is no right and wrong when holding your hook and yarn and every crocheter does it a bit differently. Generally speaking, hold your hook in your dominant hand and your yarn in your other hand in a way that makes it easy to wrap it around the hook while you hold the crochet piece you are making between your thumb and middle finger. Within these patterns I do not refer to left and right and so left-handed crocheters can follow without any alterations required, and will just be working in the opposite direction to a right-handed crocheter throughout.

MARKING YOUR STITCHES

I recommend using a scrap piece of contrasting yarn approximately 15cm (6in) long that you position through the last stitch of round 2. As you crochet through the pattern pull this yarn up through the last stitch with you so it becomes a tracking 'life line,' a little like Hansel's white pebbles, marking the last stitch in every round. The marker will weave up the fabric with you but you can pull it free at the very end and it will leave no trace. Should you need to abandon your work while you are mid-way through a round, or if you suddenly discover your stitch count is wrong at the end of a round, you'll be able to retrace your steps with your marker and avoid a total restart as you can easily back-track through several rounds.

COUNTING THE STITCHES IN A ROUND

The number in parentheses at the end of every line of the pattern is the stitch count you should have at the end of that line of instruction. If you complete a round and this number is wrong then pull the work back to your stitch marker and redo it before you progress.

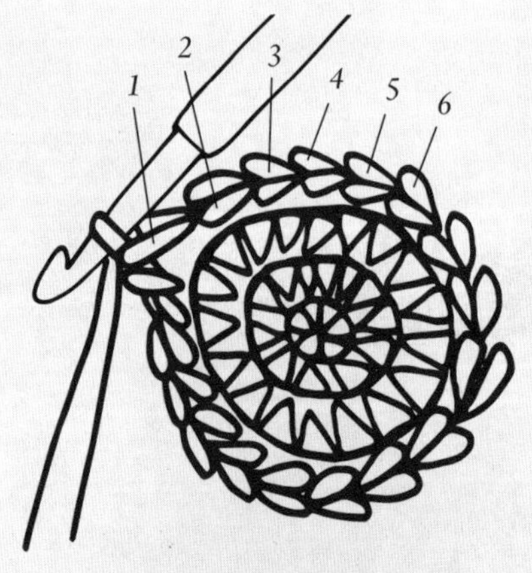

WORKING A CHAIN

When you crochet a chain and then work back down it to work a flat piece you will miss the stitch closest to the hook in order to turn. For example you might crochet 10 stitches to then crochet 8 back down.

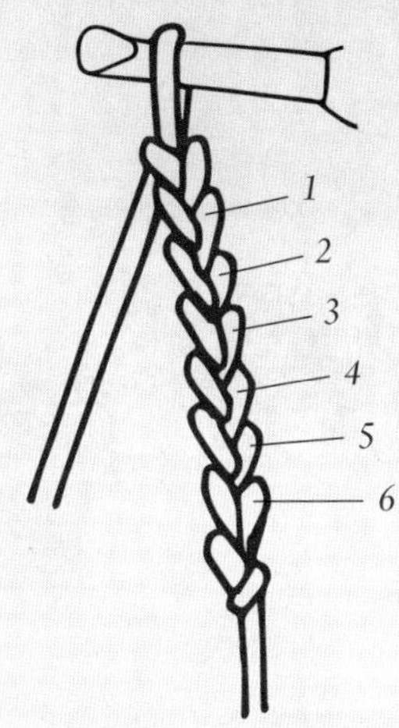

RIGHT SIDE AND WRONG SIDE

Due to generally always crocheting in one direction into the same side of the fabric, this style of crochet does have a right side and a wrong side which becomes the unseen inside of each shape. On the outside you will be able to identify your rows of stitches moving horizontally across the piece of crochet, and a foolproof method of spotting your wrong side is to take a look at your dc2togs. On the wrong side you will see the back loops of the stitches you have decreased left behind creating little lines. On the right side the decreases are almost invisible if you follow the dc2tog method stated in this book. In some patterns you will be combining both rounds and rows in the double crochet stitch. To avoid a change in stitch texture on the right side of your piece, use the invisible rows method *(see The Stitches)*.

THE STARTS

This book used three different methods for starting a new piece of 3D crochet. Sometimes you will use the 'magic ring' technique to begin a closed circular piece, sometimes you will make a chain and slip stitch it into a circle to create a large open piece, and in the third method you make a chain and crochet into either side of it to create an elongated oval-shaped start to your rounds. See full step-by-steps in *The Stitches*.

REJOINING A HOLE

On many parts in these patterns, and with the majority of feet, you will chain and miss stitches off the round leaving a hole in your piece before you later rejoin to work stitch off from the hole at a right angle. Each time rejoin with the front of the foot facing you, right-handed on the right of the hole and left-handed on the left.

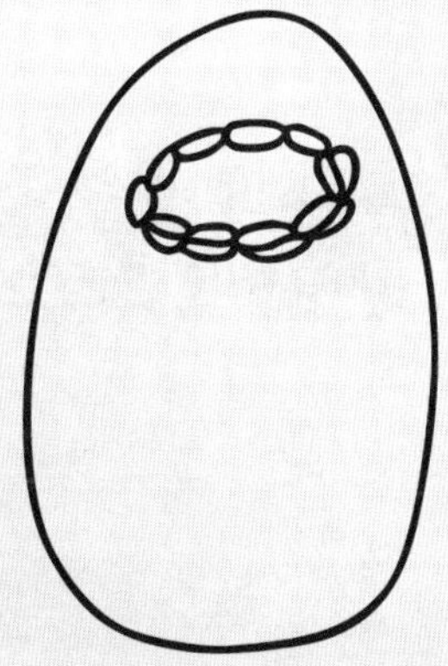

Abbreviations

The patterns in this book all use British crochet terminology and common crochet abbreviations. See *How to Use This Book* for a table of conversion to US terminology.

BP *Back post.* Work the stitch around the post of the stitch below from the back to push that stitch backwards in the fabric.

ch *Chain.* A chain is the most fundamental of all crochet stitches.

dc *Double crochet.* Using the double crochet stitch creates a compact and dense fabric.

dc2tog *Double crochet two stitches together.* Decrease by one stitch.

dtr *Double treble.* A longer more open stitch than the treble with two yarn overs before inserting hook into the stitch.

htr *Half treble.* A shorter stitch than the treble as you come through all loops after the first yarn over to end.

htr2tog *Half treble two stitches together.* Decrease by one stitch by working a half treble into the front loops of two stitches as with a dc2tog.

INV *Invisible.* This denotes a row that could be worked using the INVISIBLE ROWS technqiue should you wish to retain the same stitch texture on your fabric throught a piece.

FP *Front post.* Work the stitch around the post of the stitch below from front to bring that stitch forwards in the fabric.

FP2tog *Front post two together.* Decrease while in a rib pattern by ignoring the back post stitch and working the stitch around two front posts.

Rnd *Round.* A round is a complete rotation in a spiral back to your stitch marker. With these patterns you DO NOT slip stitch at the end of a round to make a circle, but instead continue straight onto the next round in a spiral.

Row Rows create a flat piece of fabric rather than working in spirals. When working a row turn and work immediately back into the stitch you've just worked to keep the same number of stitches on each row.

RS *Right side.* The right side of your fabric will show small 'V' shapes in horizontal lines and will form the outside of the piece of crochet.

sl st *Slip stitch.* This is the simplest crochet stitch.

st(s) *Stitch(es).* You can count your stitches around the edge of your fabric.

tr *Treble.* A longer more open stitch than the double crochet with a yarn over before inserting hook into the stitch.

ttr *Triple Treble.* A longer more open stitch than the double treble with three yarn overs before you insert your hook into the stitch.

WS *Wrong side.* The wrong side of your fabric will have vertical spiralling furrows. This is where you have all the ends or strands of yarn, and it forms the inside of the piece of crochet.

The Stitches

SLIP KNOT

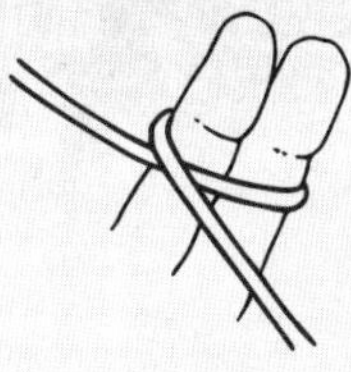

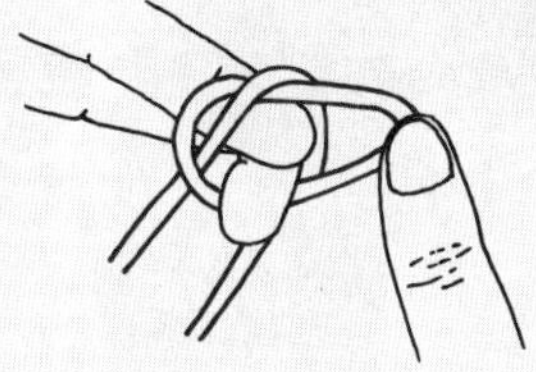

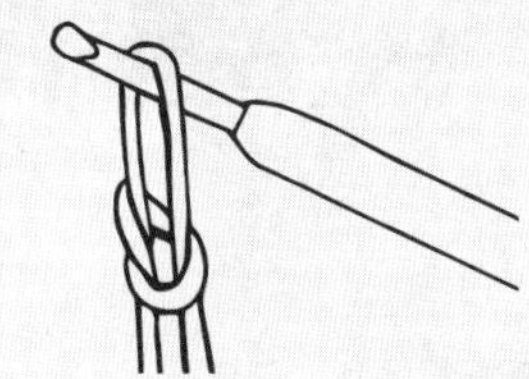

1. Make a loop in the yarn.
2. Pull yarn through the loop.
3. Place your hook through the loop and tighten.

CHAIN (CH)

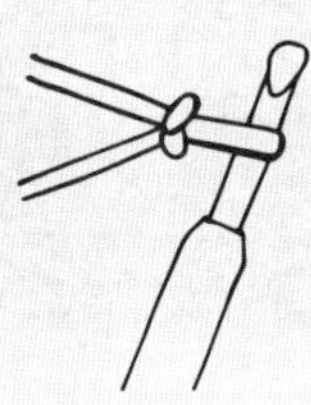

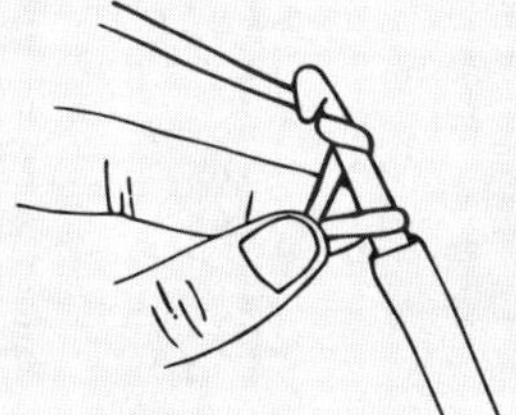

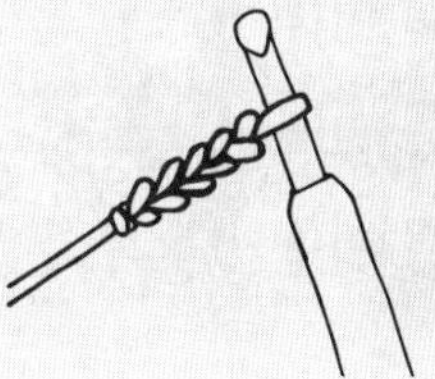

1. With your slip knot on your hook, wrap yarn over the hook (yarn over).
2. Twist the hook downwards and pull the yarn through the loop.
3. Repeat until desired length.

DOUBLE CROCHET (DC)

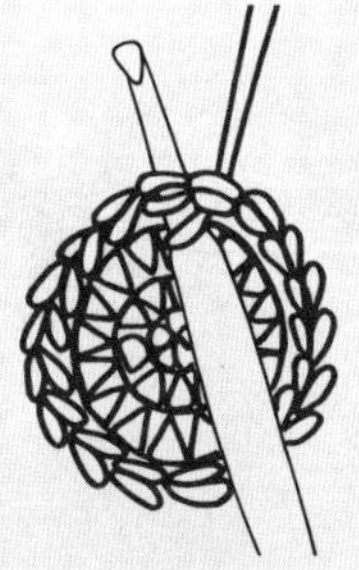

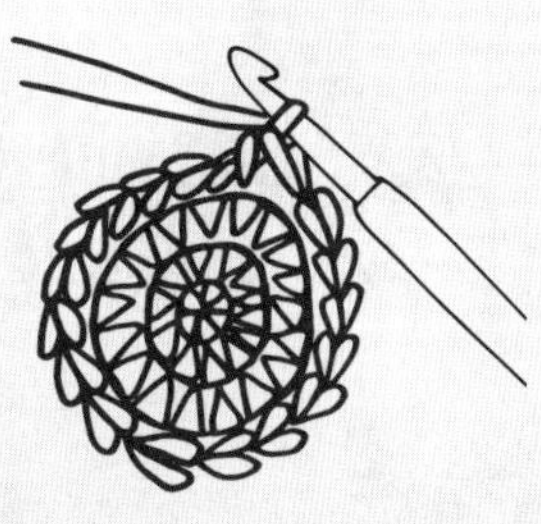

1. Insert the hook through the stitch under both loops of the 'V'.
2. Yarn over and pull through the stitch (two loops on hook).
3. Yarn over again and pull through both loops to end with one loop.

FOUNDATION RING (DC6 INTO RING)

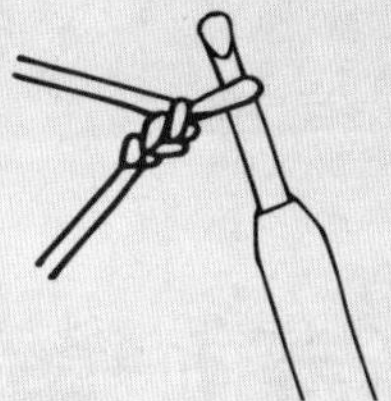

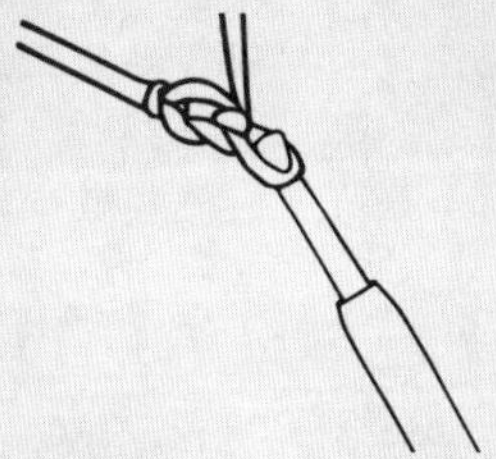

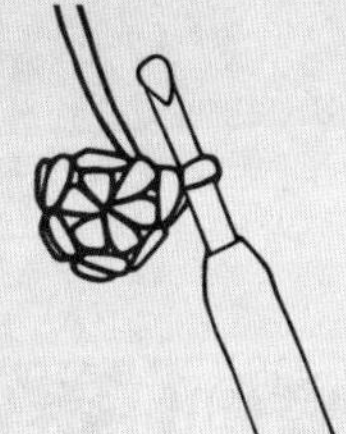

1. Make a slip knot and chain two stitches, then insert the hook into the first chain stitch.
2. Work a double crochet stitch into this stitch.
3. Work five more double crochet stitches into this same stitch to make six stitches in total. Pull tightly on the tail of the yarn to close the centre of the ring and form a neat circle.

SLIP STITCH TO JOIN INTO CIRCLE

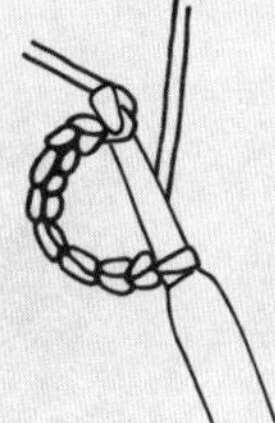

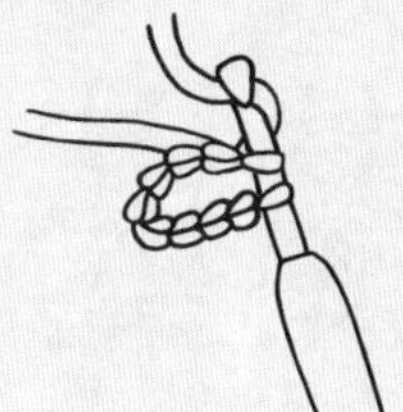

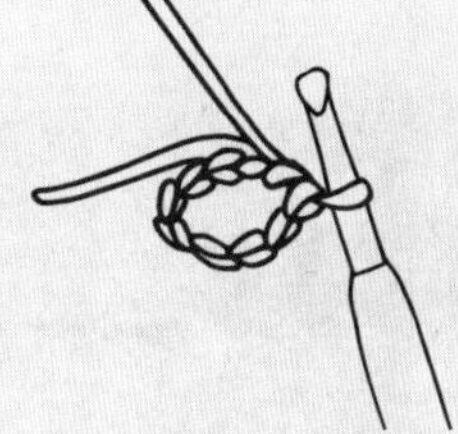

1. Chain the number of stitches stated, then insert the hook into the stitch closest to the slip knot.
2. Yarn over hook, pull the yarn through the stitch and loop on the hook in one motion.
3. Work the first stitch of the round into the last chain that you made.

WORKING AROUND BOTH SIDES OF A CHAIN TO START

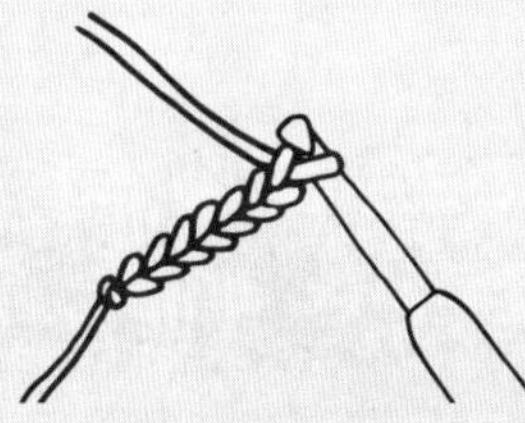

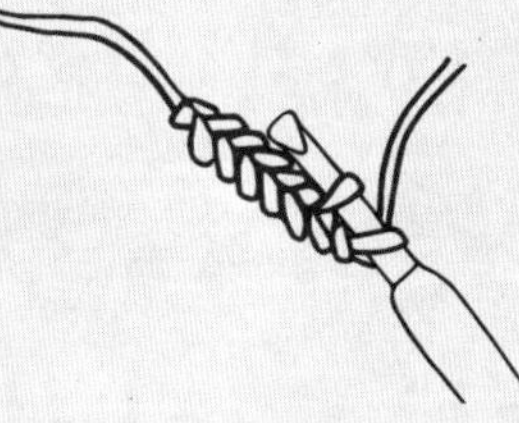

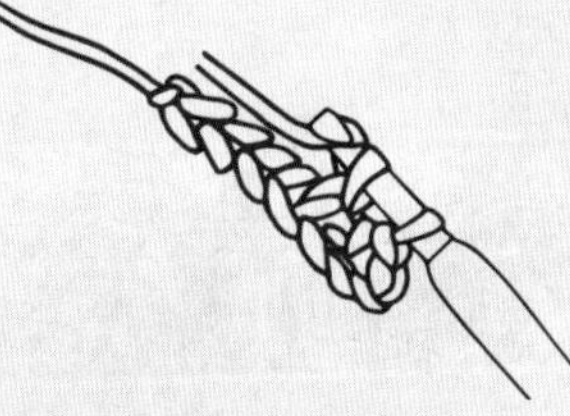

1. Chain the specified number of stitches.
2. Work the first stitch of the round into the second chain from the hook.
3. Continue working down the first side of the chain as instructed, then turn and work back up the other side of the chain to complete the first round. Place a marker.

DECREASE (DC2TOG)

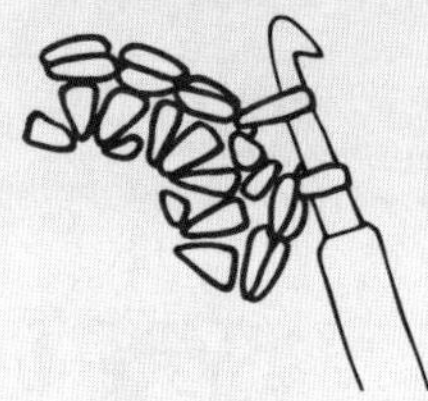

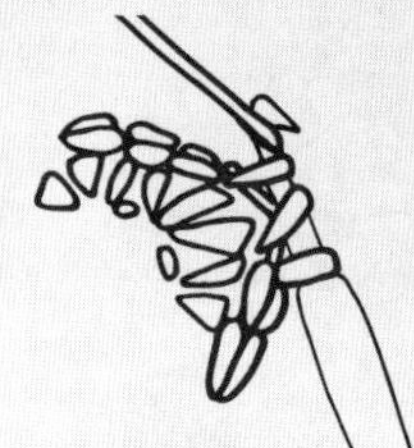

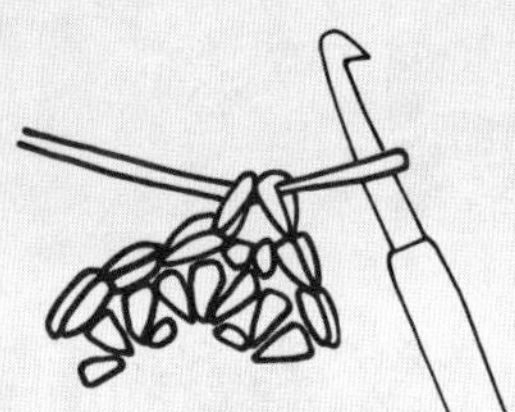

1. Insert the hook through the front loop of the stitch only (two loops on the hook).
2. Insert the hook through the front loop of the next stitch (three loops on the hook).
3. Yarn over hook and pull through first two loops on the hook, then yarn over and through both remaining loops to complete the double crochet.

CHANGING COLOUR

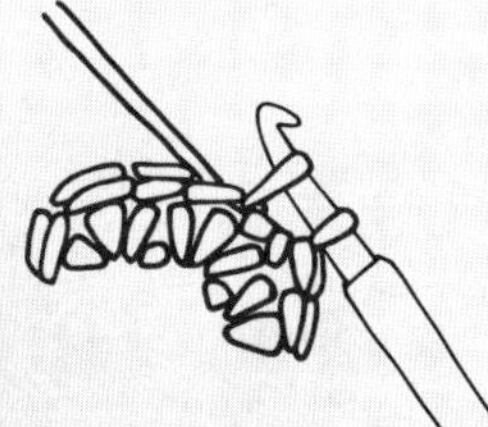

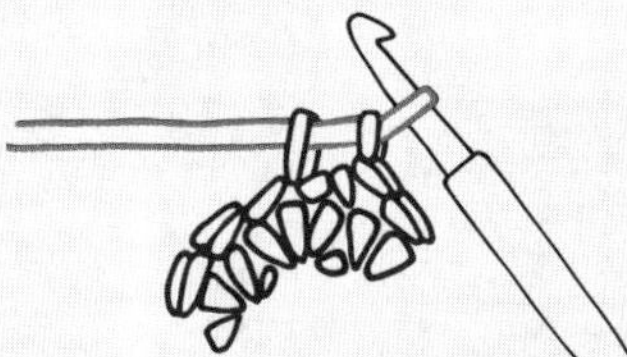

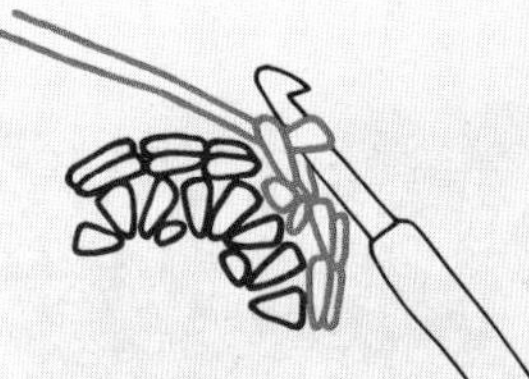

1. On your last stitch before the colour change. Insert the hook through the next stitch, yarn over and pull through the stitch (two loops on hook).
2. Yarn over with the new colour and complete the double crochet stitch with this new yarn.
3. Continue with this new colour, leaving the original colour to the back of the work. Cut if a one-off colour change or run on the wrong side of the fabric if colour changing back to it.

WORKING INTO THE BACK LOOP

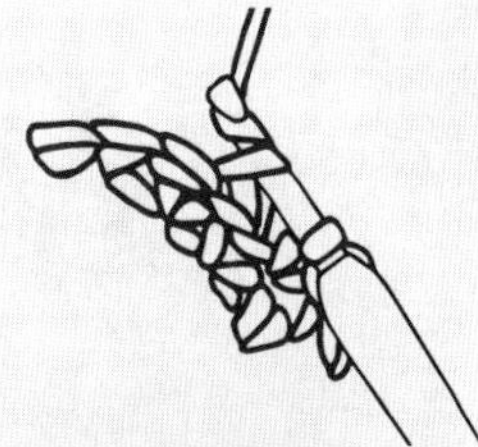

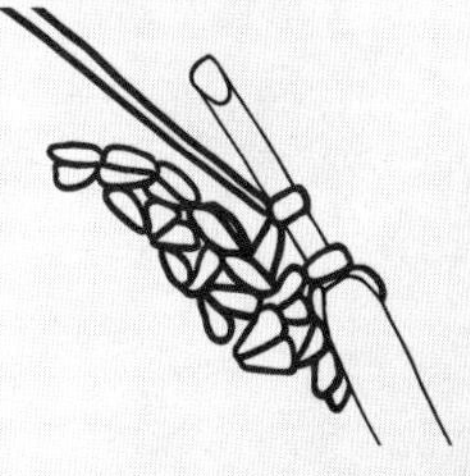

1. Insert the hook through the middle of the stitch to work the back loop only.
2. Yarn over and complete the stitch through this half of the stitch only.
3. Repeat to create a textured surface fabric as the front loops remain visible on the right side.

HALF TREBLE CROCHET (HTR)

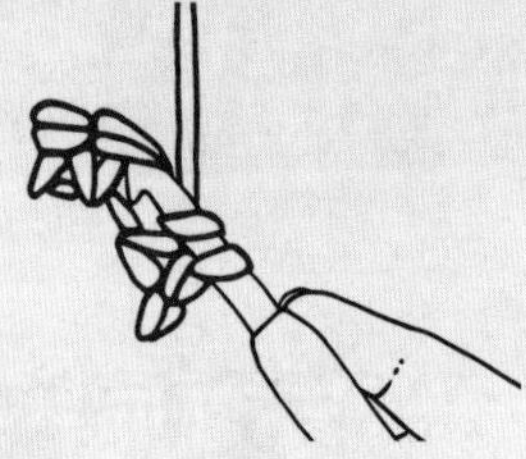

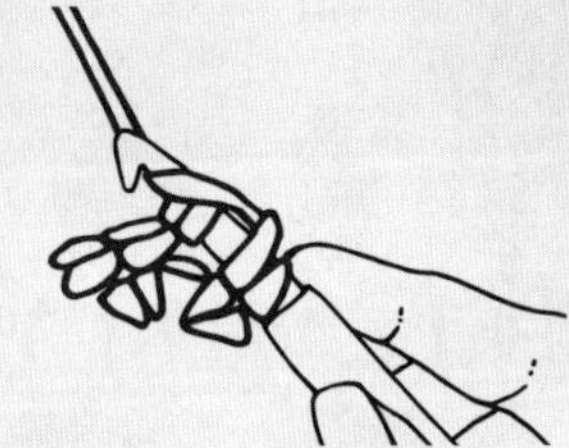

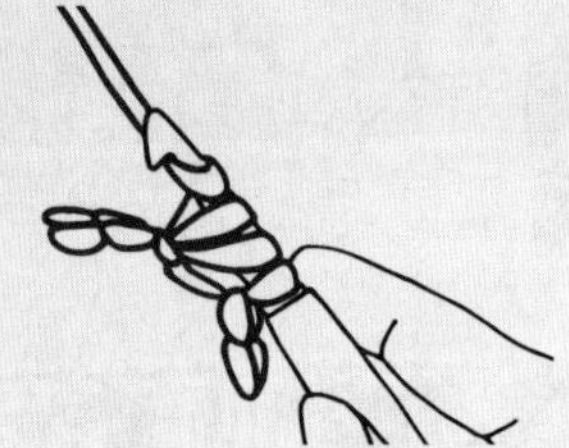

1. Yarn over and insert the hook into the next stitch.
2. Yarn over and pull through the stitch (three loops on the hook).
3. Yarn over and pull through all three loops on the hook (one half treble crochet stitch made).

TREBLE CROCHET (TR)

NOTE: for dtr and ttr add one additional yarn over at step 1 and 2

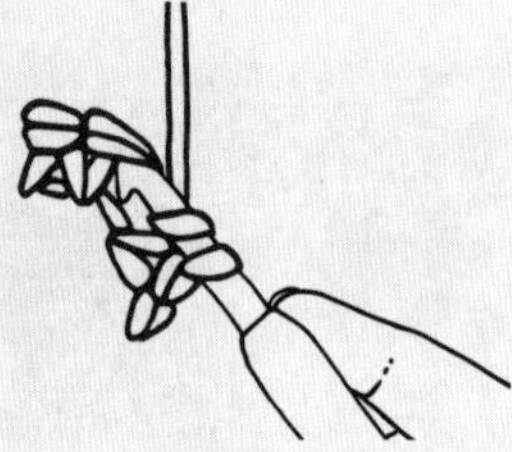

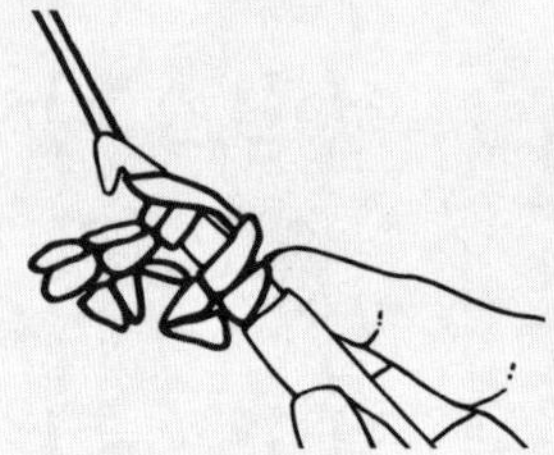

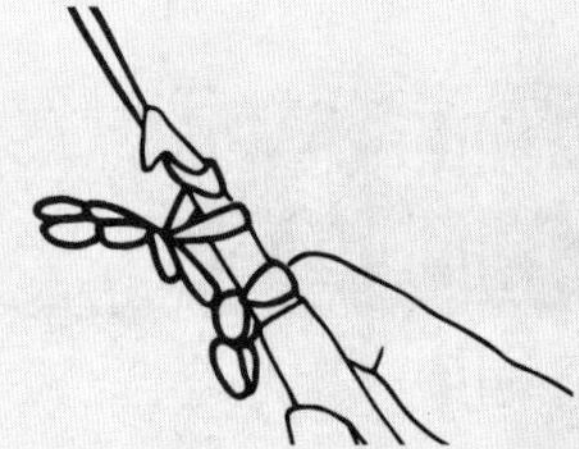

1. Yarn over and insert the hook into the next stitch.
2. Yarn over and pull through the stitch (three loops on hook), yarn over and pull through first two loops on hook.
3. Yarn over and pull through remaining two loops on hook.

SPLITTING ROUNDS

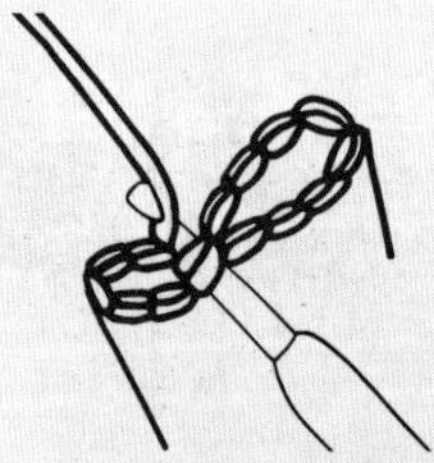

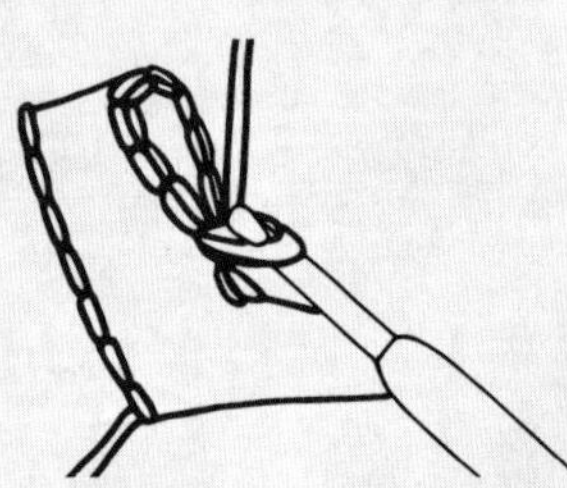

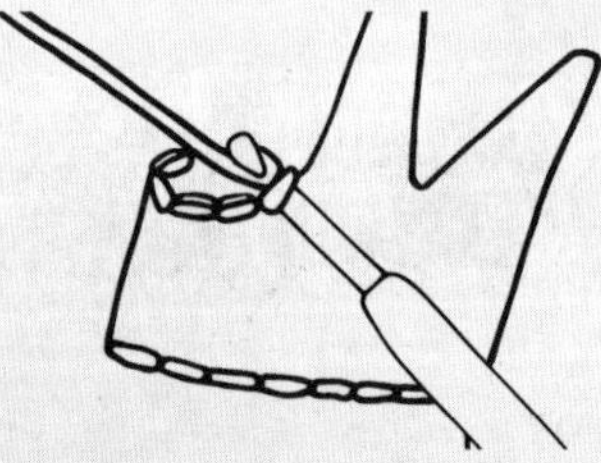

1. Count the number of stitches in new smaller round back from your hook.
2. Cross the round to double crochet into this stitch on the right side of the fabric.
3. Once you have completed this smaller round, break yarn and rejoin to work the next small round.

FRONT POST/BACK POST (FPBP)

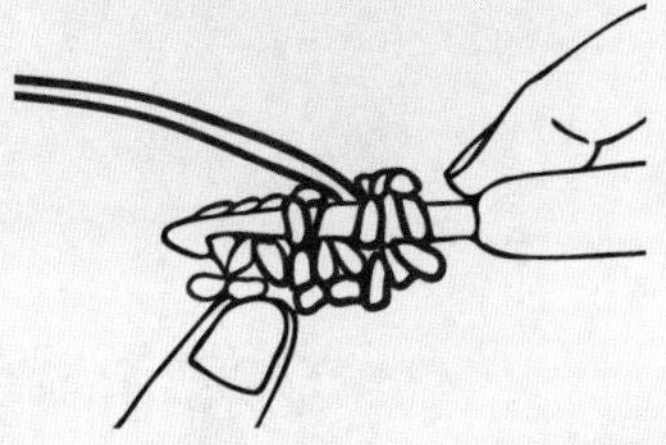

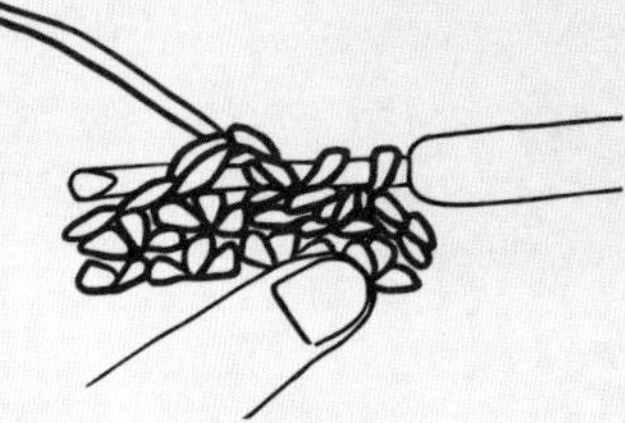

1. Yarn over, insert the hook around the post of the stitch below from front to back, pulling the post towards you. Complete st as indicated in the pattern (front post).
2. Yarn over, insert the hook around the post of the stitch below from back to front, pushing the post away from you. Complete stitch as indicated in the pattern (back post).
3. Using these two stitches alternately creates a deep rib.

SPIKE STITCH

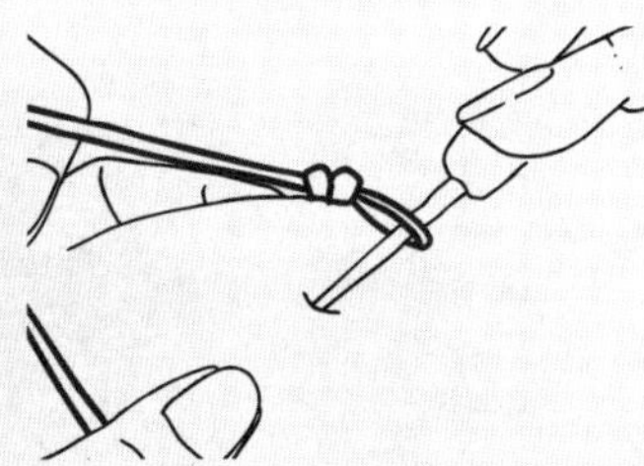

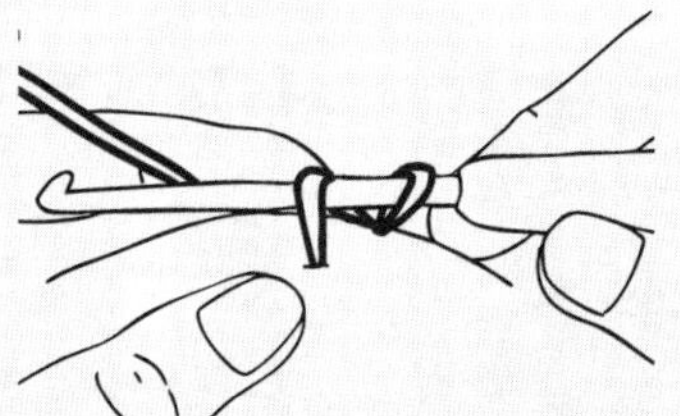

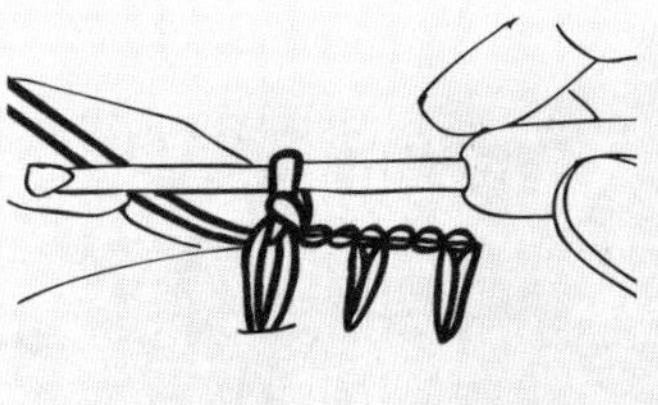

1. Insert the hook into the fabric below, beneath the next stitch you would work, as stated within the pattern.
2. Yarn over and draw the loops up to the edge of the work before completing the dc stitch.
3. Remember that this stitch replaces the stitch on the round as it overlays it.

LOOP STITCH

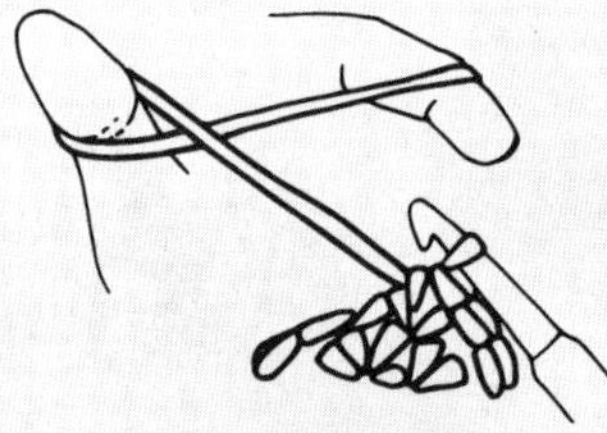

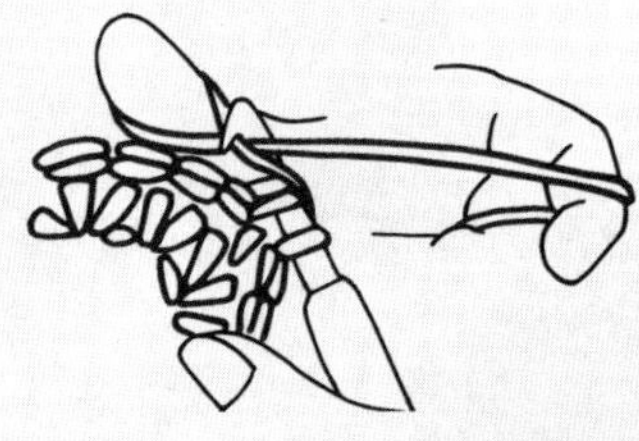

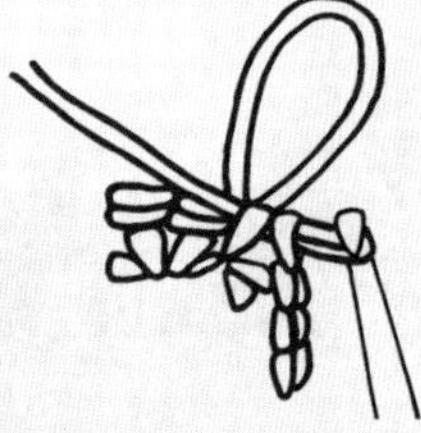

1. Insert the hook through the stitch, wrap the yarn from front to back around your thumb, yarn over and pull through the stitch.
2. Pull the loop to the front and to length stated in the pattern, then yarn over and pull through the two loops on hook to complete the stitch.
3. Repeat to work loops as often as stated in the pattern. Measure loops from the fabric to the end of the loop.

MAKE BOBBLE (MB)

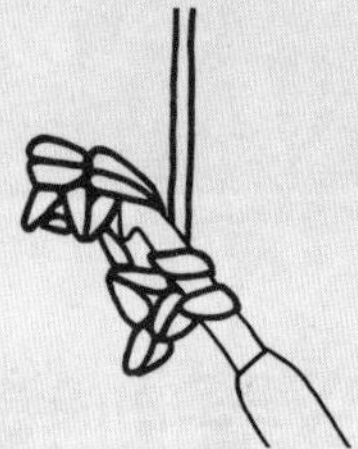

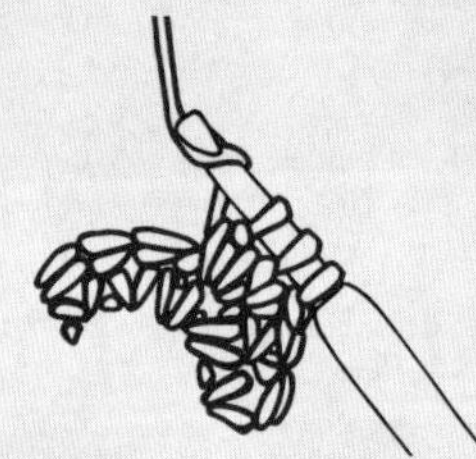

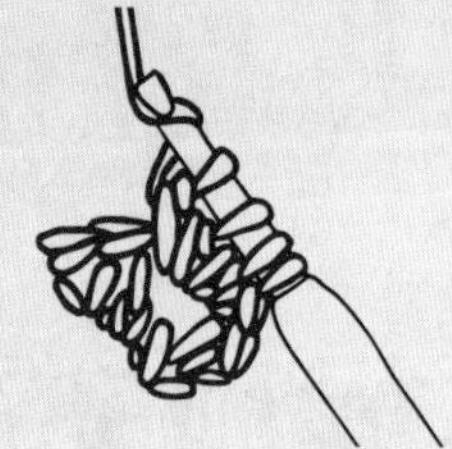

1. Yarn over and into the stitch. Now yarn over, bring back through the stitch, yarn over and back through two loops.
2. Repeat step 1 and 2 as many times as your pattern indicates. This is shown in parentheses in pattern, e.g. MAKE BOBBLE (3).
3. Yarn over and into the stitch, yarn over, bring through the stitch, yarn over and pull through all the remaining loops on hook.

WORKING ROWS

For those perfectionists out there you have the option of using the below 'invisible rows' technique whenever you work in rows to avoid the change in stitch texture that appears when double crocheting in rows rather than rounds.

There are times when extra effort of working out double crochet stitches using the 'invisible rows' technique is worth it. This allows you to crochet rows with the appearance of rounds for a consistent texture on a piece like Red Riding Hood's cape where the hood is made in rounds and the cloak itself is in rows.

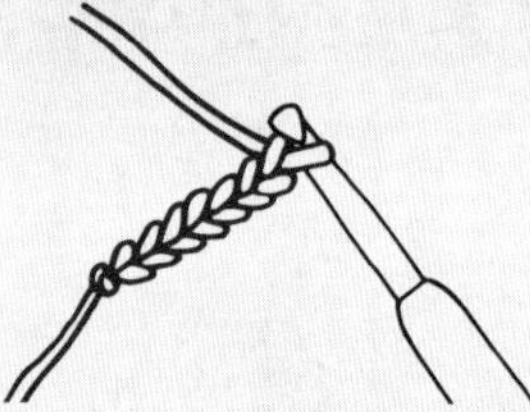

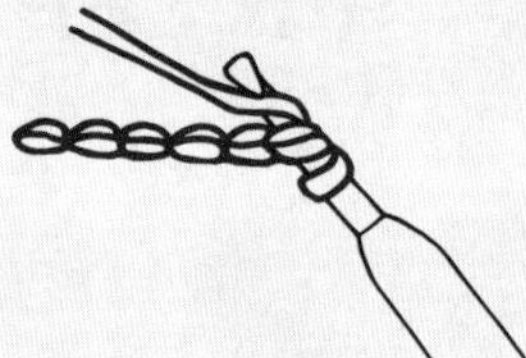

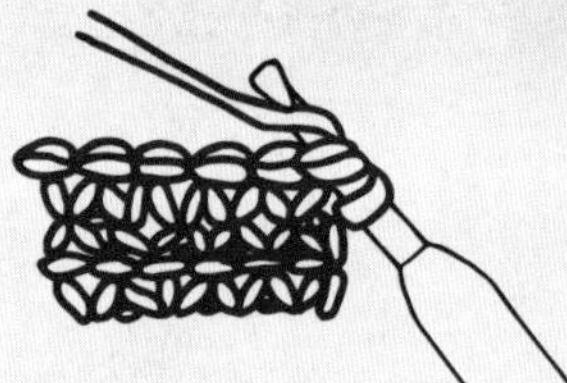

1. Chain the number of stitches stated in the pattern.
2. Starting in the second chain from hook, work back along these chain stitches to create the first row.
3. Turn piece so that the back of the previous row is facing you. Start in the first stitch next to your hook and work the next row along the row of stitches.

INVISIBLE ROWS

Working in first stitch from hook, insert hook into back of stitch towards you under working yarn, yarn over and pull through, twist last loop on hook clockwise by moving hook between loops, yarn over, pull through both loops on hook to complete double crochet. For left-handed crocheters, twist loop anti-clockwise.

Work the last stitch on the wrong side rows as non-invisible to get the neatest turn.

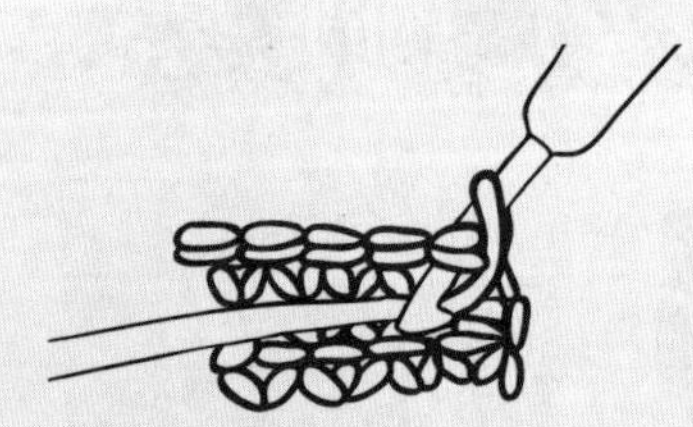

Finishing Techniques

DOUBLE CROCHET JOIN (DC JOIN)

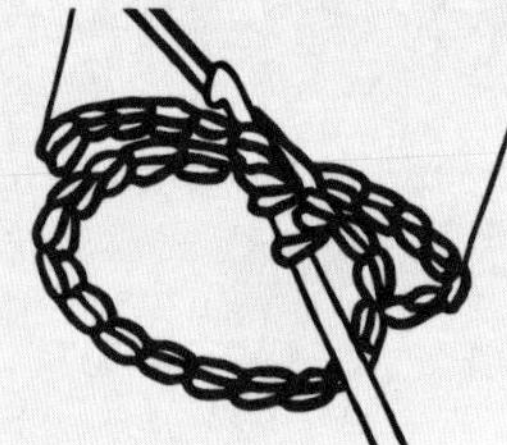

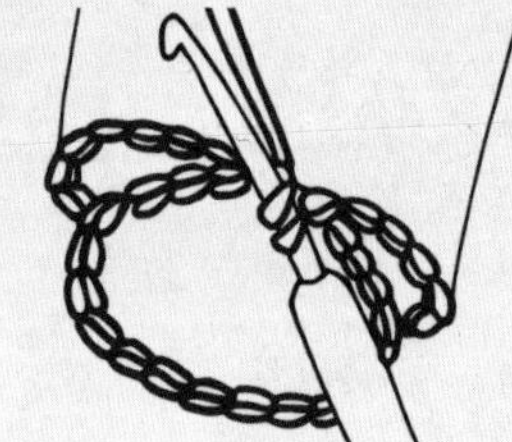

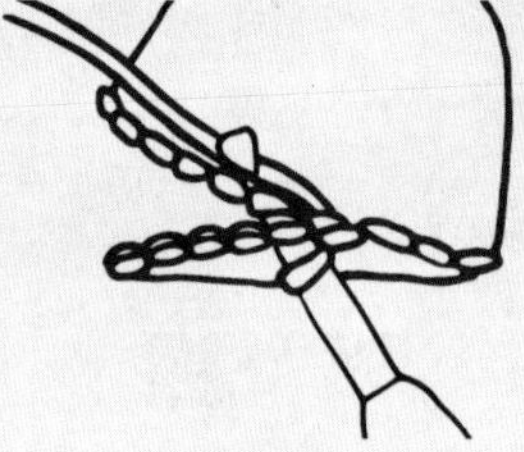

1. Insert the hook through the edge of both pieces, ensuring right sides are facing outwards. The working direction is stated in your pattern; this determines which side the edge sits on.
2. Complete your stitch through both pieces of crochet.
3. Repeat until fully joined, making sure to stuff if instructed before the work is fully closed.

SLIP STITCH TRAVERSE

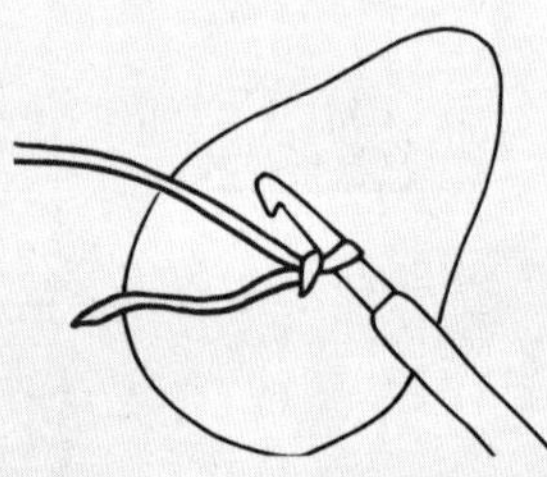

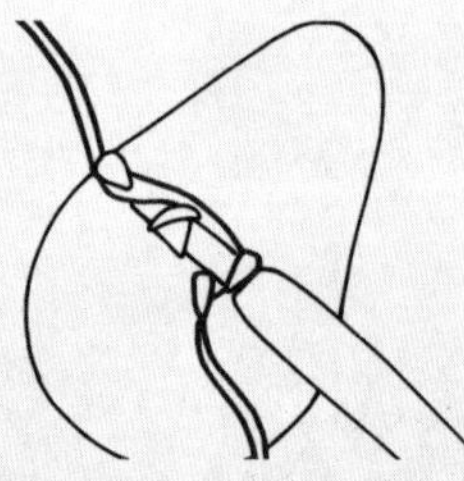

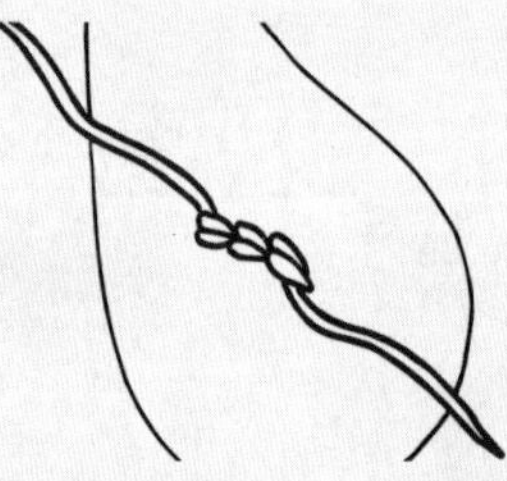

1. Insert the hook into the fabric around a stitch and yarn over.
2. Pull through the fabric and loop in one motion.
3. Continue moving across the fabric like this to reach the desired location or number stated in the pattern.

SLIP CHAINS

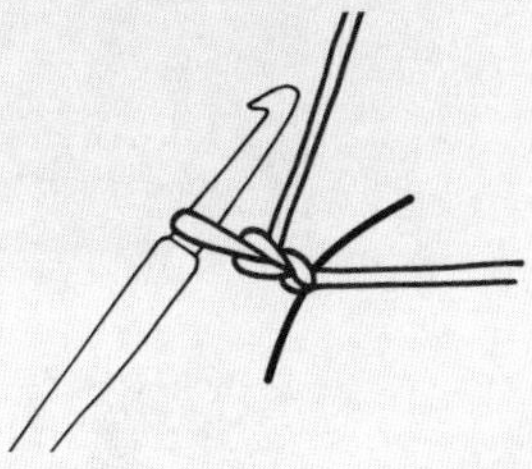

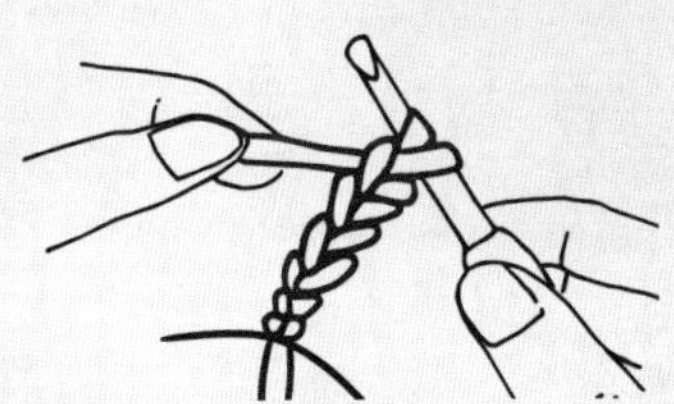

1. Insert the hook into the fabric around a stitch, yarn over and pull through the fabric.
2. Chain the number of stitches stated in the pattern.
3. Slip stitch back down the chain and then slip stitch into the fabric. Repeat as instructed.

KNOT LENGTHS

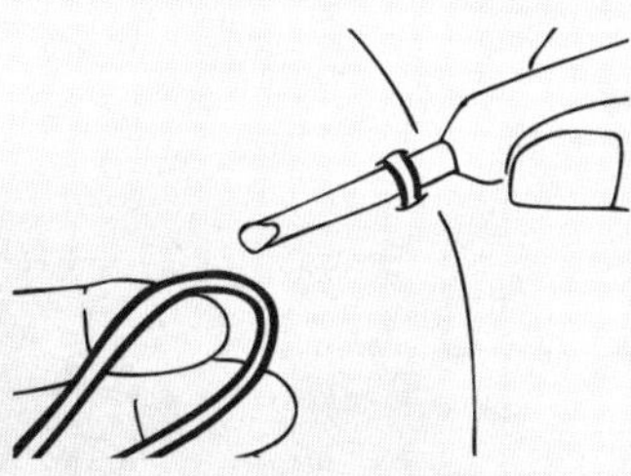

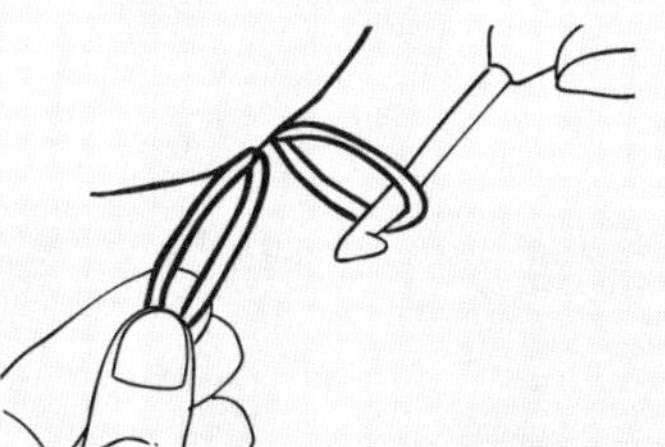

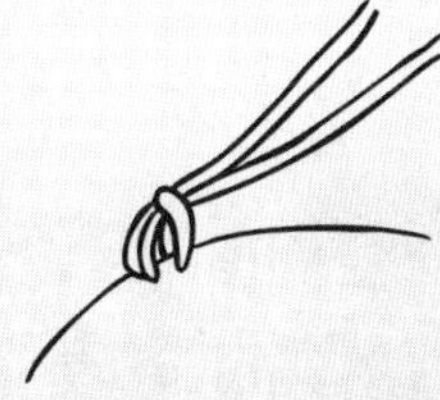

1. Cut a length of yarn and fold in half. Insert hook into stitch or fabric and yarn over with the centre of the length.
2. Bring the loop through the stitch.
3. Pull the cut ends through the loop before pulling tight to secure.

CHAIN LOOPS

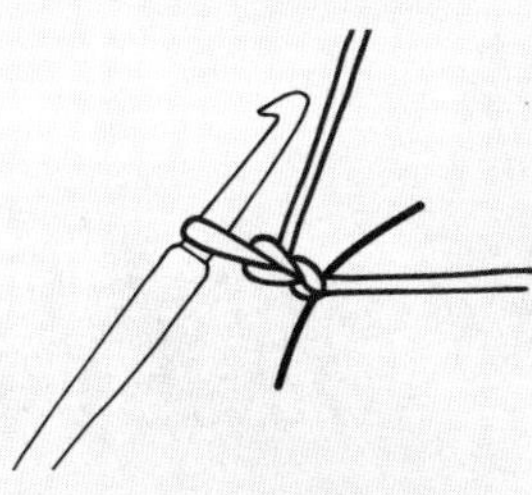

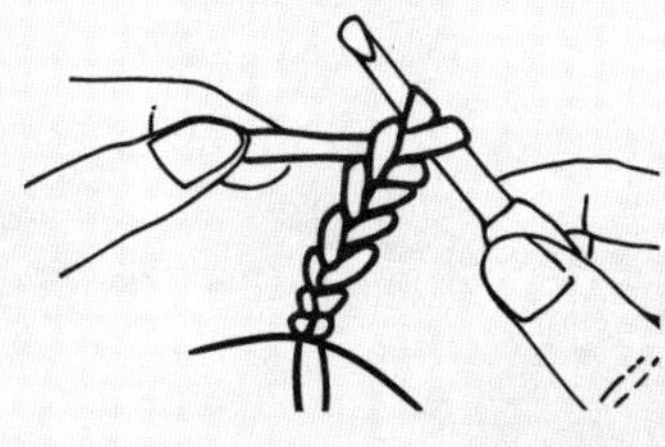

1. Insert the hook into the fabric around a stitch, yarn over and pull through the fabric.
2. Chain the number of stitches stated in the pattern, then insert hook into the fabric approx. two stitches and two rows away. Yarn over and pull through the fabric.
3. Repeat step 2 until the area is covered.

EMBROIDERY

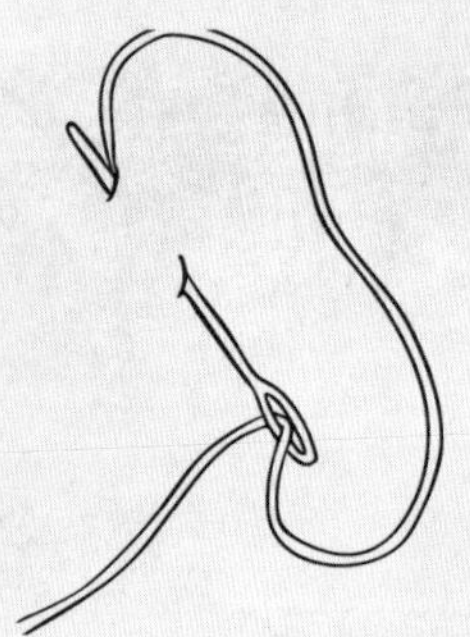

LONG STITCH

A long stitch is one straight stitch worked to any length in one direction, and is how I have always chosen to add eyes and noses to my crochet makes whether it's animal, doll or monster. For a guide to this see *Characterisation*. A long stitch can be just one wrap of yarn or can be repeated through the same start and end point to make it thicker with every additional wrap. To add texture and detail to Red Riding Hood's wolf I have used single wrapped long stitch in subtly contrasting colours inside the ears and in a triangle formation on the front and back of the torso.

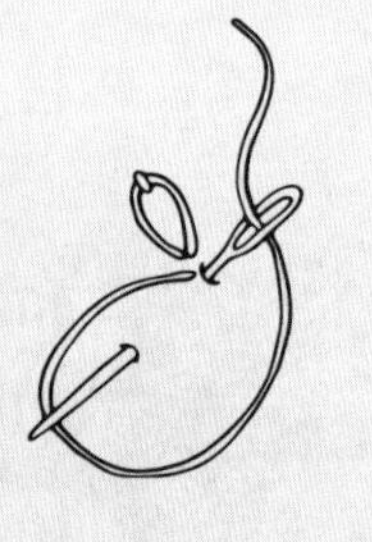

DAISY STITCH

Put the needle into the fabric where you wish the bottom of the stitch to be, and bring the needle tip out where you want the petal to end. Do not pull the needle out of the fabric at this point. Wrap the yarn around the tip of the needle and pull needle through to form a loop.

Secure into position by sewing back in just the other side of the loop.

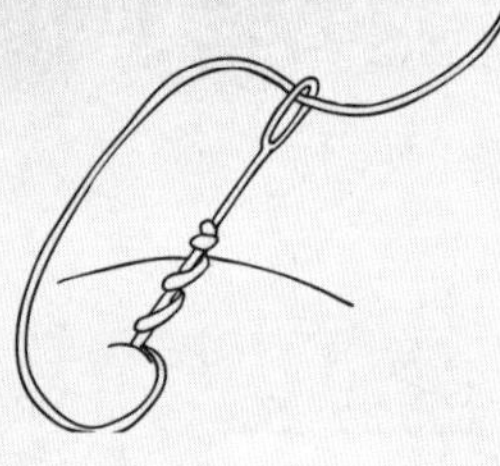

FRENCH KNOT

With yarn threaded and secured underneath, bring the needle through the fabric from underneath and pull through. Wrap the yarn around the needle four times. Insert the needle back into the fabric and pull down to create the knot.You can vary the amount of wraps to create different sized knots if desired.

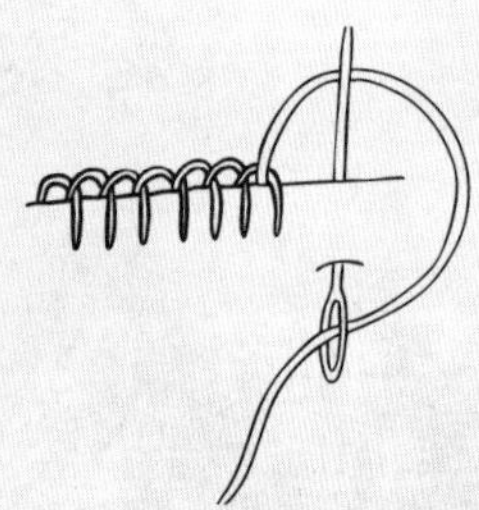

BLANKET STITCH

Secure your yarn on the back of the fabric, then working from the left for right-hand stitchers (or vice versa) push the needle through the gap between the stitches at the point at which you want the detail to end. Loop the stitching thread under the needle as you tighten the stitch then repeat two stitches away from this. This is worked best as a finishing edge to fabric.

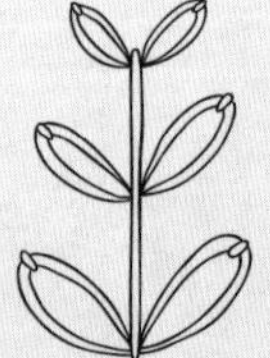

FERN MOTIF

First sew one LONG STITCH down the centre the length you wish the motif to be. Then work three pairs of DAISY STITCHES on either side of this line from the centre line outwards gradiating the lengths of them with the longest at the bottom. This embroidery motif has been used on the clothing of the Seven Dwarves in various different places to unite them.

About the Author

Kerry Lord is the founder of TOFT, a dynamic British yarn brand specialising in luxury wools and approachable patterns. Initially established with a focus on fashion-led knitting kits, Kerry first created the first edition of the very popular *Edward's Menagerie* series of books in 2012, which has encouraged and taught thousands around the world to crochet for the first time. Kerry enjoys collaborating and hosting ever-larger crochet events to bring people together that have TOFT in common, and introduce new people to the craft.

Find the videos recorded to accompany these patterns on the TOFT YouTube channel.

Thank You

This book has only been able to be conjured up from deep within my imagination due to the talent of the team who have worked alongside me. Everything from the incredibly beautiful illustrations to the photography, full layout and testing has been done by the in-house TOFT team. The magic spell to create these fairy tales has been simmering in the cauldron for a very long time at TOFT, and there was no better time for it to be realised than to celebrate our 20th year in business.

I really do feel like my three biggest wishes have been granted with the opportunity to create a book of my own fairy tales. Over the years creating these Crochet Fairy Tale books I have loved every moment of research on the project, and the task of reading every version of the stories we could find to my children has been a complete pleasure. I owe a lot of thanks to my whole family who continue to support me through my adventures into fairyland and beyond.

The talent of our head of design Rosie Collins along with the unrivalled creativity of stylist Beth Plumbley are responsible for just how beautiful this book looks. Together they also captured the magical photography that brought my crocheted fairy tales to life in a way that matched and then surpassed my imaginings of how crocheted dolls could look. The outstanding illustrations that run right across the cover and through all the pattern and story pages in this book have been penned by the very gifted Louise Humphreys. Evelyn Birch has continued to add to her TOFT technical illustrations that have now accompanied my patterns through many books, and the back of this book becomes our most extensive stitch guide to date. Without the speedy hands of Tash Jackson I would never be able to design, test and tweak enough patterns to make a full collection like this, I felt like at times I waved a magic wand and one pickaxe became seven before my eyes!

Thanks are due to Rachel Critchley who fastidiously keeps me on the straight and narrow path with the introduction of lots of new techniques and some pretty challenging new structures (not to mention all the maths!) Thank you to Yantra Taneva who applied the finishing touches to our photography. Extra thanks for her creativity also goes to Lynsey at Bake Me Happy for creating not just one but two custom gingerbread houses of our dreams working only from our illustrations.

Further thanks to Compton Marbling who were commissioned to create the unique marbling papers at the front and back combining our TOFT yarn colours and the character of these fairy tales.

A DAVID AND CHARLES BOOK

David and Charles is an imprint of David and Charles, Ltd, Suite A, Tourism House, Pynes Hill, Exeter, EX2 5WS

EU GPSR Authorised Representative:
Logos Europe, 9 rue Nicolas Poussin,
17000, La Rochelle, France
Email: Contact@logoseurope.eu

First published in the UK and USA in 2026

A catalogue record for this book is available from the British Library.

ISBN-13: 9781446316009 hardback
ISBN-13: 9781446316016 EPUB

This book has been printed on paper from approved suppliers and made from pulp from sustainable sources.

Printed in China through Asia Pacific Offset for:
David and Charles, Ltd, Suite A, Tourism House, Pynes Hill, Exeter, EX2 5WS

10 9 8 7 6 5 4 3 2

Publishing Director: Ame Verso
Managing Editor: Jeni Chown
Editor: Victoria Allen
Pre-press Designer: Susan Reansbury
Production Manager: Beverley Richardson

TOFT Team
Technical Editor: Rachel Critchley
Head of Design: Rosie Collins
Photography: Rosie Collins and Beth Plumbley
Stylist: Beth Plumbley
Narrative Illustrator: Louise Humphreys
Technical Illustrator: Evelyn Birch

David and Charles publishes high-quality books on a wide range of subjects. For more information visit www.davidandcharles.com.

Share your makes with us on social media using #dandcbooks and follow us on Facebook and Instagram by searching for @dandcbooks.

Layout of the digital edition of this book may vary depending on reader hardware and display settings.

BIBLIOGRAPHY

– *The Penguin Complete Grimms' Tales for Young and Old* Ralph Mannheim (London: Penguin Books, 1984)

– *The Oxford Companion to Fairy Tales* (Oxford: Oxford University Press, 2000)

– *Fairies and Fables* Robert Mathias (London: Hamlyn Publishing Group, 1988)

– *Grimm Tales* Philip Pullman (London: Penguin Books, 2012)

– *Hans Christian Andersen's Complete Fairy Tales* tr. Jean Hersholt (San Diego: Canterbury Classics, 2014)

– *Tales from Grimm, Andersen and Perrault* Jean Carruth (London: Purnell Books, 1976)

– *Jacob and Wilhelm Grimm selected tales* Joyce Crick (Oxford: Oxford University Press, 2005)

– *Breaking the Magic Spell* Jack Zipes (USA: The University Press of Kentucky, 1979)

– *The Complete Fairy Tales* Jack Zipes (London: Vintage Books, 2007)

– *The Hard Facts of the Grimms' Fairy Tales* Maria Tatar (New Jersey: Princeton University Press, 1987)

– *The Complete Grimm's Fairy Tales* (New York: Quarto Publishing Group, 2013)